Don't You Believe It!

Don't You Believe It!

*Exposing the Myths Behind
250 Commonly Believed Fallacies*

Herb Reich

Skyhorse Publishing

Skyhorse Publishing books may be purchased in bulk at special discounts for sales promotion, corporate gifts, fund raising, or educational purposes. Special editions can also be created to specifications. For details, contact Special Sales Department, Skyhorse Publishing, 555 Eighth Avenue, Suite 903, New York, NY 10018 or info@skyhorsepublishing.com.

www.skyhorsepublishing.com

10 9 8 7 6 5 4 3 2 1

Library of Congress Cataloging-in-Publication Data

Reich, Herb.
 Don't you believe it! : exposing the myths behind 250 commonly believed fallacies / Herb Reich.
     p. cm.
 Includes index.
 ISBN 978-1-60239-766-8 (hardcover : alk. paper)
 1. Common fallacies. 2. History–Miscellanea. I. Title.
 AZ999.R45 2010
 031.02–dc22

                                        2009032609

Printed in China

For Gerri—
my partner and co-disbeliever for almost forty-nine years,
who wore a button that read, simply, "I doubt it."

CONTENTS

Contents

PREFACE

The idea for this book first came to mind at a dinner hosted by Marty Edelston, chairman of Boardroom, Inc. Originally conceived as a series of columns for one of his newsletters, it unfortunately never quite got off the ground. Nonetheless, I credit Marty with providing the initial goad.

I had always been enthralled by the variety and quantity of garbage we carry around as seemingly usable information. In my younger days, I strained several friendships by not easily accepting the imparted intelligence of the day, rather questioning, "How do you know?" In college, I remember alienating a few professors by frequently asking "How can we be sure?" or "Where is it written and by whom?" Not so much to doubt, more to confirm. Later, I tried to instruct my daughters that things are rarely what they seem, and to guide them to question most everything, to accept nothing at face value. I apparently succeeded because they asked "Why?"

I am in debt to nameless research librarians at a number of libraries in Westchester County, notably those of White Plains, Yonkers, Mt. Vernon, Tarrytown, Dobbs Ferry, and my home base, Hastings-on-Hudson. Librarians do not always know the answer, but they do know where to look for it. My unlimited gratitude to Susan Barnett for improving the text and also spotting some grievous factual errors. A word of thanks also to David Fischer, an inexhaustible source of trivia on sports and other pabulum, this last in its good meaning. And lastly, a grateful bow to my daughter Liza for her insightful comments while critiquing the final draft of the manuscript.

FOREWORD

This is a book that will question much of what you think you know. It will look at a few hundred of the "truths" we all hold as common knowledge, that are widely accepted as fact, that are part of the body of our socially accepted data bank . . . but are simply wrong.

Our cherished culturally shared beliefs stem from a variety of sources, many of which repeat old wives' tales, myths, lore, self-serving fantasies, innocent fallacies, or sheer nonsense. History is replete with stories of great men and events that either never happened or didn't happen the way we were led to believe. These pages will reexamine several such long-held misconceptions.

Shared misinformation is common, and this book will try to correct at least some of the fallacies we've come to accept as facts. I will try to break it to you gently, but you may still be amazed at the baggage you—read "we"—have been carrying around for so long.

For example, did you know that:

- The United States did not vote for independence on July Fourth.
- The Eighteenth Amendment did not outlaw liquor.
- Red Square is not named in honor of communism.
- George Washington was not the country's first president.
- The Rough Riders did not charge their horses up San Juan Hill.
- Charles Lindbergh was not the first man to fly across the Atlantic Ocean.
- Charles Darwin didn't coin the phrase "survival of the fittest."
- Jackie Robinson was not the first African American baseball player in the major leagues.
- The Battle of Yorktown did not end the Revolutionary War.

- French fries did not originate in France.
- The clock in London's Parliament Tower is not called "Big Ben."
- Cleopatra was not Egyptian.

Have I grabbed your interest? Read on and be surprised. There is much to unlearn. Such items are part of our consensually acquired store of knowledge. They are taught in schools. They are passed down to us by our families and friends, they are part of shared cultural orthodoxy, they are accepted without question. And they are wrong.

It is appalling how much of what we take as unchallenged truth is really myth. It is a cliché that history is written by the victors. But this book will demonstrate that is also written by teachers, by reporters, by heirs, by hucksters, by word of mouth, and not infrequently by someone who has an ax to grind or simply a lousy memory.

We will touch on a number of topics—including history, current events, government, sports, geography, popular culture, and other areas of human experience—exposing errors that have been perpetuated for far too long.

The reader will also find a few items (very few) that do not strictly conform to the intent of the book, but—at least to the eye of the author—are of similar mind and offer features that are laughable, idiosyncratic, or just interesting enough to be disclosed.

We end with two short sections of quotations: one headed *Says Who?*, devoted to misattributed quotations, revealing who actually said them; the other unearthing several remarks from recognized authorities—*The Pundits*—whose foolish assertions and predictions belie their exalted positions, showing how even recognized experts all too often knew not what they were talking about. As Montaigne observed in his *Essays* over five centuries ago: "Nothing is so firmly believed as that which is least known."

The book will enlighten, and entertain. It will certainly start a number of arguments. And, one would hope, settle a few.

" . . . there is no truth to be discovered; there is only
error to be exposed."
—H. L. Mencken, *Prejudices*, Third Series (1922), Chapter 3

Don't You Believe It!

SECTION ONE:

WHAT NOT TO BELIEVE

OUR FIRST PRESIDENT

{ George Washington was the first president of our country.
Don't you believe it. }

In the formative days of our union, dating from September 1774, seven men, beginning with Peyton Randolph of Virginia, held the office of president of the Continental Congress, the first functioning government of our fledgling nation.

With the adoption of the Articles of Confederation, in March 1781, the Continental Congress officially became the "United States, in Congress Assembled," marking the beginning of transition from an alliance of colonies to a central government. John Hanson of Maryland was unanimously chosen as the first presiding officer serving a full term under the Articles. Because of his prominence in the Revolution and his influence in the Congress, other potential candidates declined to run against him. Hanson is thus considered by many historians as the first "president of the United States."

Hanson was the head of the government, presiding over Congress but without true executive powers, which were exercised by the Congress as a whole. Seven other "presidents" followed Hanson, including Richard Henry Lee of Virginia and John Hancock of Massachusetts, each serving an average of one year.

But the government under the Articles of Confederation was too inefficient for the young amalgamated country, relinquishing too much power to the several states. In response to the need for a stronger central authority, the Congress assembled for the last time in March 1789 and produced the Constitution of the United States, naming George Washington as president.

Thus, while George Washington was the first "president of the United States" under the Constitution, in actuality he was preceded by eight others who held that title.

RED SQUARE

{
Moscow's renowned Red Square (*Krasnaya Ploshchad*) was named to commemorate the victorious Communist Revolution of 1917.
Don't you believe it.
}

A colorful story, but nonetheless more myth than history. Red Square, known for the grand military displays paraded there during the Soviet era, is the legendary cobbled plaza that sits at the heart of the Russian capital. On one side is the Kremlin, with Lenin's tomb situated prominently below its redbrick wall; on the other is the enormous GUM department store. At the south end is the whimsical St. Basil's Cathedral, its world-famous onion domes dating from the sixteenth century. The north end houses the State Historical Museum with its twin pointed spires.

On the site of the old city's marketplace, Red Square has been described as Moscow's version of the Roman Forum—a vast meeting place for public functions and government pronouncements, for celebrations, for executions under several tsars, and for rock concerts by Paul McCartney, Pink Floyd, and the Red Hot Chili Peppers.

Probably the most impressive military gathering in the square took place on November 7, 1941, when thousands of Soviet troops listened to an address by Marshal Stalin and then left directly for the front lines to oppose advancing Nazi armies only one hundred miles away. Another significant event was the Victory Parade in 1945, when flags of defeated Nazi armies were victoriously displayed at the Lenin memorial.

But, contrary to popular belief, its name has nothing to do with the red of communism. The word *krasnaya* meant "beautiful" in old Russian, and "red" only more recently, originally meant to describe St. Basil's, then later applied to the entire square.

MARATHON

The modern marathon commemorates the historic run of the Greek soldier Pheidippides from the battle site in the town of Marathon to his home city of Athens in the year 490 B.C.E. His mission was to inform his fellow Athenians about their army's great victory over the Persians. The distance covered by the messenger was 26 miles, 385 yards.
Don't you believe it.

We do not know the exact length of Pheidippides' run because we have no record of the route he took, but we do know that there were at least two roads available, one about 21.5 miles, the other about 25.5 miles. Both routes are short of the conventional modern marathon distance.

When the Olympic games resumed in 1896 after a millennium and a half of inactivity (they had been abolished in 393 by the Roman emperor Theodosius I), a marathon race was included. Its length measured just under 25 miles, from Marathon Bridge to the Olympic stadium in Athens. For the first few modern Olympic meets that followed, the distance varied, ranging somewhere between 25 and 26.5 miles, requiring only that all runners follow the same course.

In 1908, the games were held in London, where the marathon course was planned out from Windsor Castle to the royal box at the Olympic stadium, a distance of 26 miles, 385 yards. The marathons run in the next few Olympics in other cities again covered differing distances, but in 1921 the London measure was adopted by the International Amateur Athletic Commission as the official marathon length and was used in the next Olympic Games in 1924 in Paris.

That distance has now been formally established as the standard and has remained the course length of marathon races in and out of the Olympics ever since.

BURNING WITCHES

{
During the witch hunt frenzy of the late seventeenth century, several witches were burned at the stake in Salem, Massachusetts.
Don't you believe it.
}

It is surprising to learn that not one "witch" was put to the torch as a result of the infamous Salem trials in 1692. In the hysteria of the period, more than one hundred people in that vicinity were accused of practicing witchcraft. Extant documents relating to the Salem trials reveal that in the months June through September, thirteen women and seven men were executed—nineteen by hanging, and one, Giles Corey, pressed to death by having increasingly heavy stones piled upon his chest. In addition, several others died in prison while they were awaiting execution. But not one accused person in Salem died by fire.

The witch hunt had started in Europe in the fourteenth century, an adjunct to the brutal Inquisition by which the Catholic Church hoped to eliminate all heretics—that is, people who didn't conform to church teachings. It was most active between 1450 and 1700, with witchcraft high on the church's list of heresies. Heresy was a crime in most of Europe, the penalty for which was typically torture until the accused confessed.

Those accused found themselves in a paradoxical situation. Since it was virtually impossible to refute the accusation of witchcraft, the best chance to avoid torture, once charged, was to confess and to suffer the punishment.

The Inquisition eventually came to an end by the late seventeenth century, closing a sad period in European history, an era during which it is estimated some five hundred thousand people were executed throughout Europe. But in England and the colonies, contrary to common belief, not one accused witch was burned at the stake.

POST OFFICE MOTTO

> *Neither snow nor rain nor heat nor gloom of night stays these couriers from the swift completion of their appointed rounds.*
>
> It is generally accepted that this statement represents the proud motto of the U.S. Postal Service.
>
> **Don't you believe it.**

Although the aphorism is frequently cited as the tenet of our mail carriers, in actuality the USPS has no official motto. The lines quoted above are those inscribed on the General Post Office in New York City at 8th Avenue and 33rd Street, known as the James A. Farley Building in honor of the Postmaster General under F.D.R. from 1932 to 1940. But the lines do not constitute an administrative precept of the USPS.

The misconception is in fact so common that the USPS has felt the need to post a disclaimer on its official Web site, offering the following explanation:

> This inscription was supplied by William Mitchell Kendall of the firm of McKim, Mead & White, the architects who designed the New York General Post Office. Kendall said the sentence appears in the works of Herodotus and describes the expedition of the Greeks against the Persians under Cyrus, about 500 B.C. The Persians operated a system of mounted postal couriers, and the sentence describes the fidelity with which their work was done. Professor George H. Palmer of Harvard University supplied the translation, which he considered the most poetical of about seven translations from the Greek.

So while our mail deliverers may take pride in these sentiments, and may strive to live up to the stringent code expressed in this inscription, it is not the official doctrine of the U.S. Postal Service.

Arnold Rothstein and the Black Sox Scandal

{ Gambler Arnold Rothstein fixed the 1919 World Series. **Don't you believe it.** }

Contrary to what Hyman Roth (Lee Strasberg) tells Michael Corleone (Al Pacino) in *The Godfather, Part II* ("I've liked baseball ever since Arnold Rothstein fixed the 1919 World Series"), Rothstein did not hatch the plot for the infamous 1919 Series in which the Chicago White Sox intentionally lost to the Cincinnati Reds. The Chicago team was thereafter referred to as the Black Sox, a nickname obviously meant to disparage them.

The scenario was devised by the players themselves, led by first baseman Chick Gandil. For several seasons, the team members had been chafing under the management of Charles Comiskey, owner of the Chicago team, who had, among other provocations, reneged on the payment of promised bonuses. The players felt underpaid and undervalued and were readily amenable to a scheme that would both embarrass Comiskey and provide them some easy money.

Rothstein was brought in long after the conspiracy was hatched. Other gamblers preceded him in the cabal, but none could supply the cash required to engage the players. Always alert to the opportunity to turn a quick illegal buck, Rothstein realized the potential of cashing in on a predetermined outcome. Rothstein did furnish the capital needed to make the plot possible, but he was not one of the instigators.

Rothstein served as financier of the machination, not as prime provocateur, although he later also provided some muscle to convince recalcitrant players to stay in the fold.

As a result, eight players and several gamblers were indicted for conspiracy, but Rothstein was not among them. All were acquitted for lack of evidence, several transcripts of confessions having gone astray from the court files.

DR. MUDD AND JOHN WILKES BOOTH

The government unjustly convicted Dr. Samuel Alexander Mudd of complicity in the assassination of President Abraham Lincoln. When Dr. Mudd provided medical care to John Wilkes Booth, he had no idea who Booth was.
Don't you believe it.

Just as a refresher: In attempting to escape after shooting Abraham Lincoln in Ford's Theatre, John Wilkes Booth broke his leg leaping from the presidential box. He was nevertheless able make his getaway on horseback, traveling some thirty miles south to arrive at the home of Dr. Samuel Mudd in the predawn hours. Dr. Mudd set Booth's broken leg and helped him on his way.

Dr. Mudd was later arrested and eventually convicted of conspiring to help Booth assassinate Lincoln and to aid his escape. Mudd proclaimed his innocence, arguing that he hadn't known Booth but was simply helping a traveler in need.

After serving almost four years of a life sentence, Mudd was pardoned by President Andrew Johnson in February 1869. Mudd later achieved the status of folk hero, believed by many to have been an innocent victim of an overzealous government.

The record, however, reveals that Mudd, an advocate of slavery, may not have been the guiltless naïf that he claimed to be. Despite his denial, Mudd had met Booth at least twice before the night of his medical aid, once even providing Booth with overnight accommodations in his home. Earlier, Mudd had been instrumental in organizing with Booth a group planning to kidnap the president in order to boost the Confederate cause.

Historians have traced the course of Mudd's anti-Lincoln activities, detailing his part in the kidnap plot and charting his meetings with the conspirators. Although he has been clearly implicated in the kidnap scheme, historians do believe that Mudd was not involved in planning the assassination.

GRAVE ROBBERS

{ Grave robbers defile what should be inviolable sites, and by doing so they have proven to be a scourge of society.
Don't you believe it. }

Grave robbers may have provided an unsuspected legacy to today's medical knowledge.

Until about the thirteenth century, medical training consisted of sedentary lecturers verbalizing theories, most of which were fallacious, frequently based on long-standing myths and erroneous assumptions rather than on practical experience. Such was the case in the teaching of anatomy. The idea of actually looking inside a human body was unheard of. Even Galen, the second-century anatomist who was still the leading authority, had derived his knowledge from dissecting lower animals.

Then, in the 1400s, medical education began including dissection of human corpses in a new, realistic approach to anatomy. But even then, students were not allowed hands-on participation. Typically, the teacher sat and lectured while a barber did the cutting and students observed. Not for several hundred years thereafter were students themselves permitted to do dissections.

But as the practice spread, it became harder to obtain bodies for teaching. Enter the grave robbers, or resurrectionists as they were called, who by the eighteenth century turned a good profit supplying bodies for physicians to study. They robbed the graves of the poor and unclaimed, those who were least likely to be missed. Some took their practice a bit far, as witness the notorious Burke and Hare, who committed several murders to procure corpses for sale.

So, absent those who took the career too seriously, grave robbers may actually have contributed to medical understanding.

SURVIVAL OF THE FITTEST

{ In *The Origin of Species*, Charles Darwin introduced the concept known as "survival of the fittest." **Don't you believe it.** }

Yes, he did discuss the principle, but that is not what he called it. Darwin analyzed the concept in great detail, but referred to it as "natural selection." The term "survival of the fittest" is nowhere to be found in his original 1859 publication, or in any of its subsequent three editions.

The expression was provided by Herbert Spencer, a philosopher contemporary with Darwin, in his *Principles of Biology* in 1864. Spencer found the phrase descriptive of an economic process—parallel to that of biological evolution—by which companies adapt to the marketplace in order to increase their ability to grow and prosper.

Darwin liked Spencer's term because it eliminated the troublesome implications in the word "selection," and he adopted it in the 1869 fifth edition of *Origin*, wherein he wrote: "I have called this principle, by which each slight variation, if useful, is preserved, by the term natural selection, in order to mark its relation to man's power of selection. But the expression used by Mr. Herbert Spencer, of the Survival of the Fittest, is more accurate, and is sometimes equally convenient."

The phrase has since been used to describe the dynamics of a variety of other competitive activities analogous to evolution. However, it has drawn criticism from some authorities, who disapprove of it as a tautology meaning simply "survival by those most prepared to survive," and thus adding nothing to our understanding of the process. Nonetheless, the term has survived because it seems a fitting characterization of many situations.

EIGHTEENTH AMENDMENT

{ The Eighteenth Amendment to the Constitution— proposed by Congress on December 18, 1917— prohibited the consumption of alcoholic beverages. **Don't you believe it**. }

The Eighteenth—or, as it was popularly known, the Prohibition Amendment—made no restriction on drinking or possessing liquor, or on serving it to friends, or even to mere acquaintances. Nor was the purchase of alcoholic beverages declared illegal. All it prohibited was "the manufacture, sale, or transportation of intoxicating liquors" used for "beverage purposes." Under the amendment, it was illegal to sell liquor but not against the law to buy it or own it.

Nor did the amendment define what "intoxicating liquors" were. That was left to the National Prohibition Act (popularly known as the Volstead Act, not to be confused with the constitutional amendment) which defined an offending potable as any beverage that contained at least one-half of 1 percent of alcohol by volume. The Volstead Act—which was passed in October 1919, becoming effective on February 1, 1920—went beyond the amendment to extend the ban to purchase or possession. Medicinal application was excluded, as was sacramental use in religious rites. The Volstead bill had been vetoed by President Wilson, but his veto was overridden by Congress.

The amendment, after approval by thirty-six states, was declared ratified on January 29, 1919, and remained in effect for almost fifteen years. It was finally repealed by the Twenty-first Amendment, which was adopted December 5, 1933.

And, one bit of collateral information—which imbibers will laud but prohibitionists will grieve—the Eighteenth was the only constitutional amendment ever to be repealed.

HORATIO ALGER, JR.

The American Dream—the possibility of achieving success and fame through hard work and virtuous living—is forever associated with the writings of Horatio Alger, Jr., who no doubt shared the good fortune of his characters.

Don't you believe it.

Alger wrote more than one hundred novels, most about street urchins who achieved success by a strict work ethic and a life of moral probity. Though his books are now fading into obscurity, his inspirational message—to try harder and to want more—persists in the national psyche.

However, Alger's own life was nothing like that of the characters in his novels. As a child, he developed nearsightedness and asthma and suffered poor health for the rest of his life. He was unsuccessful at almost everything he tried, and he considered himself an abject failure. The son of a fanatically religious father, Alger graduated from Harvard University, edited a Boston periodical, served slightly over a year as a Unitarian minister (he was removed, charged with "unnatural familiarity with boys"), owned a failed curio shop, fell short at writing adult fiction, floundered as a playwright, made vain efforts to create a children's theater, had few friends, never married, sired no children, had two unsuccessful love affairs—one with a married woman—and in general was unable to cope with the demands of daily living.

But his inspirational books were read by millions of teenaged boys, who saw within the pages their chance of escaping their lowly status and climbing the ladder of success.

The irony was that this man whose literary creations offered a vision of advancement for hard work, who heralded hope and evoked images of fame and fortune—this man who promoted the American Dream—died in poverty.

HENRY HUDSON

{ Hendrik Hudson was a Dutch explorer who discovered the Hudson River.
Don't you believe it. }

His name was not Hendrik, but Henry; and although he sailed for the Dutch East India Company, he was not Dutch. He was English.

Historians know little about Hudson, except that he seems to have been obsessed with finding a passage to the Orient. It is known that in 1607, on a ship named the *Hopeful*, he tried unsuccessfully to sail to China from England via the North Pole. In 1608 he tried, again in vain, to find a Northeast Passage. In 1609, sailing now for the Dutch East India Company as captain of the *Half Moon*, he tried once again to find a passage to the East, this time by following the north coast of Russia. But his crew mutinied, preventing him from pursuing a Northeast Passage, so he attempted instead to find a Northwest Passage. He reversed course and sailed across the Atlantic, exploring the coasts of North America and probing the river that bears his name.

His next and last voyage ended in disaster. An autocratic master, he lost control of his crew after a winter of extreme hardships; they mutinied and abandoned him and his son on land bordering what is now called Hudson Bay, where he may have died. There his record stops; no one knows what happened to him after that fateful journey.

But one thing is known: He did explore the river that was named for him, but with no interest in the river per se. When he realized it wasn't the passage he was seeking, he abandoned the search. However, he can't be credited with being the first European to sight the river. That honor goes to Giovanni da Verrazano, an Italian navigator in the service of France, who explored the North American coast in 1524.

CAESAR AND BRUTUS

> Marcus Junius Brutus, he of the Roman Senate, one
> of Caesar's assassins, was in reality Caesar's son.
> **Believe it if you will. It is unlikely but possible.**

It was well known in Rome that Caesar had a long-standing affair with Servilia, Brutus' mother, and many in Rome suspected that Brutus was born of that relationship. Authorities do not know exactly when Servilia became Caesar's mistress, so the relationship's timetable is unclear. They further observe that Caesar would have been only fifteen years old when Brutus was born, thus throwing doubt on Caesar's paternity, but not totally discounting the possibility. In his *Life of Brutus*, Plutarch does reveal that Caesar "in his youth had been very intimate with [Servilia], and she passionately in love with him."

In the popular mind, Caesar's last words are those from Shakespeare's reenactment of Caesar's assassination, when he says, "Et tu, Brute," meaning "You also, Brutus." This has been popularly interpreted as Caesar's dismay at being repudiated even by one of his most trusted friends. But the Roman historian Suetonius has reported Caesar's utterance, somewhat differently, as "You too, my child." If quoted accurately, these words could support belief of Caesar's paternity. Of course, the line might suggest an emotional rather than familial kinship, so even here the implication is vague. Some writers have interpreted it to mean, "Your turn is next."

As is the case with so many historical events, authorities are not certain of the details. There is no definitive record of what Caesar said at his assassination if, indeed, he said anything. But the experts do find agreement on one datum, that he was stabbed twenty-three times. (History seems to have a selective memory.)

Was Brutus Caesar's son? In the absence of accurate family records or clear DNA evidence, we will never know. But the question does offer an intriguing speculation.

ROPE

{
Alfred Hitchcock's 1948 film *Rope* is a landmark in
cinema history, known as the first and only time an
entire film was shot in one continuous take.
Don't you believe it.
}

The film—based on a 1929 stage play, *Rope's End*, by Patrick
Hamilton—was a dramatization of a sensational Chicago murder
case of the 1920s. A fourteen-year-old named Bobby Franks had
been killed by two brilliant but deviant acquaintances, late-teen
pampered rich kids Nathan Leopold and Richard Loeb, who
sought the intellectual thrill of demonstrating that they could get
away with murder. The screenplay, penned by Hume Cronyn and
Arthur Laurents, had to skirt around the play's manifest homosexual relationship between the two murderers, which offended
the Production Code of the time, and had to imply the homo-
eroticism rather than making it explicit.

Lauded by some critics, dismissed as trivial by others, the film
remains an oddity within film history, badly flawed in its drama-
turgy but displaying Hitchcock's technical mastery.

As for the film being one continuous shot, such a feat would be
an impossibility in that the standard film canister of the time held
only about ten minutes of film, requiring the reel to be changed
every time ten minutes were recorded. What appears to be one
continuous take was achieved by Hitchcock in a bit of cinematic
subterfuge. He shot each canister without a break or change of
perspective, ending with the camera settling momentarily on a
full-screen dark image—either an actor's back or someone crossing
in front of the lens. At that point the reel was changed and the
action continued apparently uninterrupted.

So while the film appears to be a continuous real-time event,
it is in truth composed of ten separate takes pieced together in a
technically flawless integration.

THE HESSIANS

{
The Hessians were German mercenaries hired
by Great Britain to fight the colonists during the
American Revolutionary War.
Don't you believe it.
}

The true story is not quite that straightforward. The German
soldiers who fought on the side of the British were not what we
usually think of as mercenaries. Rather than soldiers-for-hire,
their ranks were made up of petty criminals, debtors, drunkards,
and other undesirables who were impressed and conscripted into
German regiments. They were, in effect, leased to the British by
the rulers of several German principalities, some of which were
actually subjects of King George III. The Hessians were needed
to fill the ranks because George simply couldn't raise enough
soldiers for his own army to fight the Americans, having already
committed forces elsewhere against France, Spain, and Holland.

More than half of the thirty thousand troops shipped here
from the Continent were from the principality of Hesse-Kassel
and so all became known as Hessians. Frederick II, leader of
Hesse-Kassel, was well paid for these troops, while the soldiers
received very little, if anything at all, some earning no more than
their daily rations of food.

Since they were sent to the colonies mostly against their
will, defections were common, and once here the soldiers discovered a thriving German segment of the American populace,
which tended to dampen their combative ardor. Nonetheless,
most Hessian regiments acquitted themselves well, both in their
discipline and their fighting skill.

After the hostilities ceased, an estimated five thousand
German soldiers settled here rather than return to their comparatively second-rate life back in their homeland.

FIRST AFRICAN AMERICAN IN MAJOR LEAGUE BASEBALL

{ Jackie Robinson was the first African American baseball player in the major leagues.
Don't you believe it. }

Robinson was the first in the modern era, but the first African American team member in the majors was an Ohioan named Moses Fleetwood Walker, who played catcher with the Toledo Blue Stockings in the 1884 season.

Attractive, intelligent, and an outstanding athlete, at twenty Walker had enrolled in Oberlin College, a liberal arts school known for admitting African American and women applicants. Aside from his studies, he spent most of his extracurricular time on the baseball diamond. In 1881, his senior year, Oberlin fielded its first varsity baseball team and Walker quickly became a major force on the roster. A year later he entered the University of Michigan law school, where he also played varsity baseball and was soon recognized as a star of the team.

In 1883 "Fleet" signed on as catcher with the Toledo team, then part of the minors' Northwestern League. The following year Toledo joined the American Association, one of three major baseball leagues of the time, and Walker played in his first major league game on May 1, 1884, against the Louisville Eclipse. Two days later he got his first big-league hit. Later in the season Walker's younger brother Welday also joined the Toledo squad as a replacement outfielder. Baseball historians accept the Walker brothers as the two earliest African Americans in the major leagues.

On the field, Walker was often disparaged by opposing players and jeered by the fans. A notable antagonist was future Hall of Famer Cap Anson, known for his racial intolerance, who once refused to play against Walker "because of his color."

In July, having played in forty-two games and hitting .263, twenty-three points above the league average, Fleet sustained a season-ending injury. The Toledo team folded at the end of the year, but Walker came back in 1885 with Cleveland and then several other minor league squads until he retired from the Syracuse team in 1889, shortly before organized baseball unofficially banned African American players.

In 1891, Walker was assaulted by several white men on a street in Syracuse, New York, and in the melee he stabbed and killed one of his attackers. Charged with second-degree murder, he was tried and acquitted by reason of self-defense.

Embittered by his experiences both on and off the field, in 1908 Fleet Walker published a pamphlet titled *Our Home Colony: A Treatise on the Past, Present, and Future of the Negro Race in America,* in which he argued for black emigration back to Africa as a response to racial prejudice.

But he did set the stage for the heralded arrival of Jackie Robinson some sixty years after him.

(Recently, William Edward White, a student at Brown University, was revealed to have substituted in one game for the Providence Grays on June 21, 1879, five years before Walker. But White's qualification is uncertain: he was only a stand-in, not a regular team member, and was the son of a white father and a biracial mother. It should be remembered that at the time a person would be considered black if only one of his progenitors was African American even three or four generations back. News articles of the time indicate that contemporary reporters, unaware of his racial background, assumed he was white.)

DR. SEUSS

{
Theodor Seuss Geisel, a.k.a. Dr. Seuss, is thought to
have been a real doctor in his nonliterary life.
Don't you believe it.
}

Mr. Geisel, a product of Springfield, Massachusetts, attended Dartmouth College and England's University of Oxford, preparing for a career as an English professor. But his creativity led him on a different path. The "Dr." in his pen name is a tribute to his father, who had hoped that the son would complete a doctorate at Oxford. Seuss was his mother's maiden name.

His flair for writing developed early; he became a regular contributor to Dartmouth's humor magazine, *Jack-O-Lantern*, and soon was contributing cartoons and humorous articles to such magazines as *Judge* and *Vanity Fair*. During World War II Seuss' political cartoons became well known, many displaying strong support for President Roosevelt's leadership in the war. He also made training films for the military. Along the way, he was the recipient of several major prizes, including a Pulitzer, a Peabody Award, two Emmys, and two Academy Awards, one in 1947 for Best Documentary—his *Design for Death*, a study of Japanese culture—the other in 1950 for Best Animated Short Subject, *Gerald McBoing-Boing*.

But his most lasting influence grew out of his singular knack for making reading fun for children in such international favorites as *The Cat in the Hat*, *Green Eggs and Ham*, *Hop on Pop*, and *How the Grinch Stole Christmas*. All were made more appealing by his repetitive use of simple language and his outrageous illustrations.

Incidentally, although we have become accustomed to pronouncing his name rhyming with "Juice," his stated preference was more Germanic: "Seuss—rhymes with voice."

BUNKER HILL

"Don't fire until you see the whites of their eyes."
A stirring wartime entreaty memorializing a historic battle early in the Revolutionary War. The command, which every schoolchild has been taught, was reputed to have been issued by Colonel William Prescott to his volunteer militiamen as British troops stormed the fortified American position on Bunker Hill.
Don't you believe it.

It was June 17, 1775, during the siege of Boston. Colonial forces, having locked the British into the city, learned that the redcoats planned to occupy several surrounding hills as a prelude to breaking the siege. Ahead of the British, a revolutionary garrison had been assembled on the Charlestown Peninsula, a strategic area that overlooked both Boston and its harbor and offered a vantage point for artillery fire on the city.

Throughout the previous night the militiamen had labored to build a defensive fortification. In the morning, General William Howe led the attacking troops, which were repulsed twice by the hill's defenders, who inflicted devastating losses on the British regulars. On their third assault, however, the seasoned British soldiers successfully broke through the colonists' breastwork and overran the small fort and the assembled colonial volunteers. But theirs was a Pyrrhic victory, the king's forces suffering more than 1,000 casualties of their force of 2,200.

Although the Americans lost the battle, they showed for the first time that they could stand up to the best of the British army, a force superior in numbers, training, equipment, and experience. Which makes for a glorious page in American history—except for a few details: The Battle of Bunker Hill was not fought on Bunker Hill, but farther down the peninsula on Breed's Hill. And no one knows which American commander issued the order.

ST. PATRICK

{
Saint Patrick is the patron saint of Ireland. So he must
have been of Irish descent.
Don't you believe it.
}

Little is known reliably about the life of St. Patrick. Even his
dates are uncertain. He was born in 385. He was born in 387. He
died in 461. He died in 493. Authorities differ on his significant
dates as well as other pertinent data. But we do know that he was
not born in Ireland and did not have Irish parents.

Actually, Patrick was born in what is now Scotland to a
well-to-do Christian family of Roman heritage. He exhibited
no interest in religion in his youth. When he was about sixteen
he was captured by a band of Irish marauders and sold to an
Irish chieftain for whom he served as a shepherd. During this
formative period he spent considerable time learning the local
language and customs. He escaped after six years and began traveling throughout the continent.

Several years later he started his studies for the priesthood,
and in 433 he returned to Ireland on a mission to convert the
"heathens" to Christianity. Opposed by the Druids, Patrick traveled throughout Ireland, building churches and converting thousands. Although the exact dates of his activities are clouded in
mythology, it appears that his mission lasted some thirty years
and was extremely successful; by the time of his death virtually all
of Ireland had become Christian. In about the eighth century, he
became the patron saint of Ireland.

Although most scholars now consider as folklore the stories
of his driving the snakes from Ireland and his using a three-leafed
shamrock to explain the Trinity, St. Patrick—though not of Irish
blood—is still honored as the personification of Ireland.

CLEOPATRA

{ Cleopatra—the fabled Queen of Egypt, divine Ruler
of the Nile, Monarch of Alexandria—was obviously
an Egyptian.
Don't you believe it. }

Cleopatra was a descendent of Ptolemy I, a Macedonian Greek and general in the army of Alexander the Great. On the death of Alexander in 323 B.C.E., Ptolemy became satrap of Egypt, which Alexander had wrested from Persian control. In 305 B.C.E. Ptolemy declared himself king, thus beginning the 275-year period when Egypt was ruled by Macedonian Ptolemys, the dynasty of a bloodline kept "pure" by several incestuous brother-sister marriages.

Cleopatra's father, Ptolemy XII Auletes, was a drunkard and libertine known for his cruelty and sexual promiscuity; her mother is unknown, more likely a concubine than a queen. When Ptolemy XII died in 51 B.C.E., he left his throne jointly to his eighteen-year-old daughter, Cleopatra VII (almost all Ptolemic women were named Cleopatra), and her younger brother, Ptolemy XIII. Their joint rule was not harmonious; rather it was marked by mutual open hostility.

When the Roman legions arrived in 48 B.C.E., Cleopatra saw Caesar as her hope of solidifying her power. To that end, she was soon engaged in what history records as a torrid love affair with Caesar. After Caesar's death in 44 B.C.E., she later enticed and married another Roman leader, Mark Antony.

Following his defeat by Octavian in the naval battle at Actium in 31 B.C.E., Antony committed suicide and soon thereafter so did Cleopatra, bitten, as the story goes, by the well-known asp.

Thus ended the rule of Cleopatra, whom the *Encyclopedia Britannica* labels as "the prototype of the romantic femme fatale," the Egyptian queen who possessed no Egyptian blood.

CHARLES LINDBERGH

{ It is popular knowledge that Charles Lindbergh made the first nonstop flight across the Atlantic Ocean. **Don't you believe it.** }

The first nonstop transatlantic flight was made in June 1919 by two British World War I pilots, Captain John Alcock and Lieutenant Arthur W. Brown, flying a Vickers Vimy bomber from St. John's, Newfoundland to Clifden, Ireland, covering 1,960 miles in sixteen hours and twelve minutes.

A month earlier, a U.S. Navy-Curtiss NC-4 flying boat, piloted by Coast Guard Lieutenant E. F. Stone, with a crew of five navy men aboard, had made the very first transatlantic flight. But it was not accomplished as a single stage; between its departure from Rockaway, New York, and its arrival in Lisbon, Portugal, it touched down at Newfoundland, the Azores, and other intermediate locations. The 4,526-mile trip took place over a period of twenty days, but encompassed only fifty-three hours and fifty-eight minutes of flying time.

Lindbergh's contribution to aeronautical history was as the first nonstop *solo* flight across the Atlantic; a 33.5-hour journey beginning on May 20, 1927, from the U.S. mainland (Roosevelt Field, New York) and ending on the European mainland (Le Bourget Field, outside Paris)—a total of 3,600 miles. His craft, named *The Spirit of St. Louis*, was a Ryan monoplane powered by a lightweight Wright Whirlwind engine.

Lindbergh later wrote about his feat in a 1927 book, *We*, the title referring to himself and his plane. He later used the name of the plane as the title of his 1953 autobiography, which earned a Pulitzer Prize.

Just for the record, the first woman to fly nonstop, by herself, across the Atlantic was Amelia Earhart, in May 1932, flying from Newfoundland to Northern Ireland.

PLUM PUDDING

> Probably the best known of all the "stupid questions"
> is: "What was the color of George Washington's
> white horse?" But try this one: "What fruit is in plum
> pudding?" Easy answer?
> **Don't you believe it.**

As every accomplished cook knows, plum pudding may use several fruits: raisins, currants, apples, and, in some recipes, even figs—but never plums. Included is the peel or juice of lemons and oranges, often citron—but never plums. Even cognac, rum, or other spirits may be added—but never plums.

Then why is the dish named plum pudding?

The name—and the dish—dates back several centuries. Traditionally served as part of the Christmas feast, this rich dessert has a long history as a holiday staple. In medieval times, prunes (i.e., dried plums) were a common ingredient in pies and puddings, but by the sixteenth and seventeenth centuries they were gradually replaced by raisins. The ingredients changed, but the name persisted, and still today this particular savory is known as plum pudding. The confusion even crept into the then developing language: in his famous dictionary, Samuel Johnson employed the word "plum" to mean raisin, or dried grape. Customarily in England, small silver charms or silver coins were baked into the pudding.

The richness of plum pudding is legendary; so much so that, in Oliver Cromwell's Puritan England, plum pudding, along with its cousin mincemeat pie, was banned as "sinfully rich" and "unfit for God-fearing people."

Over time, the dish has lost its popularity, probably because of the extended time required to prepare it. But it still appears in the British culinary pantheon and is well worth the tasting for those who never have enjoyed it.

BIG BEN

So you're off to London with maps and a guidebook listing landmarks not to be missed. High in your "must-see" inventory are Buckingham Palace, Westminster Cathedral, the Tower of London, and Big Ben.

The palace, the cathedral, and the tower are all easily found in different parts of the city, and you can readily see Big Ben rise above the Parliament building.

Don't you believe it.

Not that Big Ben's closed for renovation or obscured by London's notorious foggy weather. It's simply not exposed to the sightseeing tourist. The reason is simple: Big Ben is neither the 316-foot-high clock tower (properly called St. Stephen's Tower) that is attached to the eastern end of the Houses of Parliament building; nor is it the world-famous four-sided clock in the tower. Big Ben, in reality, is the name of the largest bell in the tower chimes, which, behind the walls of the tower, is not in view even from any of the best vantage points.

The original bell was cast in August 1856, but could not be positioned in place because the tower had not yet been completed. In the interim, the bell was mounted in the Palace Yard at Westminster, where it cracked beyond repair in the process of being tested. The metal was then melted down and recast in April 1858 into the present bell. Measuring nine feet wide at its greatest diameter, seven-and-a-half feet high, and weighing thirteen-and-a-half tons, it is named for Sir Benjamin Hall, who was commissioner of works when the bell was installed. It is rung every hour on the hour and is accompanied by four smaller bells, each chiming at quarter-hour intervals.

So unlike the admonition to the unruly child, Big Ben can be heard but not seen.

Mourning Black

{ The color black is the universal symbol for mourning. **Don't you believe it.** }

The color symbolizing mourning, like the particular colors associated with other aspects of human activity, varies widely between cultures. Black is the color of mourning for most Americans and Europeans, and was also used by the ancient Romans and Egyptians. But this is not so in other parts of the world. In Japan and China, for example, white is the color of mourning, although blue is frequently worn for Chinese funerals. In fact, in China, black is the color for young boys.

In India, black is considered an unlucky color; mourning is represented by the color brown because it resembles dying leaves. In South Africa red is the color of mourning, while in China red represents good luck and in Russia it stands for beauty (in Russian the word *krasnaya* means both red and beautiful) and it also represents communism.

Blue is the mourning color in Iran, while in ancient Egypt blue was worn by the pharaohs to ward off evil; in Western societies, feeling blue describes a state of unhappiness. In modern Egypt and Myanmar, yellow is the color of mourning, while in dynastic Japan warriors wore yellow chrysanthemums to symbolize their courage.

Violet, which is worn by widows in Thailand to mourn their husbands' death, was also the color of mourning in Tudor Britain and represents death in Brazil. In Central America, the color of marigolds is associated with death, and the flower is frequently used as a grave decoration.

Thus, the meanings of colors—including those used traditionally for mourning—have strong cultural differences in various parts of the world.

DIAMONDS

{ Diamonds are so expensive because they are a scarce commodity.
Don't you believe it. }

Although millions of dollars are spent each year to project this image of the diamond, it is decidedly not true. The availability and price of these "precious" stones are not subject to the usual market dynamics of supply and demand. Rather, both supply and demand are strictly controlled by the De Beers Corporation of London and South Africa, a very efficient cartel that oversees the availability of the stones and their price. By manipulating the market, De Beers is able to bypass the customary forces that determine valuation.

It is estimated that several billion dollars' worth of the stones are in storage, released on a schedule that implies their rarity and maintains their high marketplace cost. Their value is thereby artificially inflated.

Diamonds had been a scarce commodity until the middle of the nineteenth century when they were discovered in South Africa, at which time large quantities became available and the price fell significantly. Soon thereafter, following a concerted effort to acquire claims, the newly created De Beers Mining Company became the major owner of the mines and thus controlled a large share of the stones uncovered. By the mid 1930s, De Beers had become the prime mover in the diamond market, largely able to regulate prices and manage the supply.

Since then, De Beers has further strengthened its grip on the diamond industry and now virtually controls the exclusive distribution of the stones throughout the world. As new reserves have been discovered in various countries, De Beers has brought them into the syndicate, permitting the company to maintain and even expand its worldwide diamond-market control.

To forestall a secondary market in used stones, which would increase supply and decrease prices, De Beers produced an ad campaign promoting the slogan, "Diamonds are forever," cleverly suggesting that diamonds have heirloom status and are not meant to be sold but to be passed down to descendants. The point was to keep previously owned stones off the market so as to minimize the potential competition to De Beers from their greater availability.

De Beers' monopolistic practices have brought it into conflict with American antitrust laws that have barred it from retailing its products in the United States. Still, De Beers acts as the clearinghouse for most of the world's raw diamonds. For several years now, the American government has been trying to penalize the company for its closed market policies. But inasmuch as the company is headquartered in a different country, the American government's authority has been limited.

In 1994 the Justice Department brought suit for price-fixing of industrial diamonds, mostly in the United States. That suit was settled in July 2004 when De Beers SA pleaded guilty and agreed to a $10 million payment. The overall feeling was that De Beers settled the suit because it could no longer ignore the U.S. market in light of the growth of newer suppliers and the development of synthetic diamonds.

But probably the strongest influence in the demand for diamonds has been in their advertising. Well crafted and insidiously creative, diamond promotion has proven extremely effective, offering the ultimate luxury item of devotion. To men, the ads imply, "Buy her a diamond and she'll jump into your bed," to women, "He doesn't really love you until he buys you a diamond—more so if he buys two."

So while diamonds are promoted as the ultimate expression of love, they are really a marketing ploy—thought by many to be the biggest scam of the last hundred years.

QUICKIES

{ Here follows a gaggle of popular misconceptions, all self-explanatory, and requiring no exegesis. }

A football is not pigskin. It's made of cowhide.

A baseball is not horsehide. It's also made of cowhide.

When Juliet asks, "Wherefore art thou, Romeo?", she's not asking where he is, but rather, in the meaning of the time, why he is doing what he's doing.

Bone china actually does contain bone. Calcified animal-bone ash adds to the durability of the product.

Henry Ford is thought to be the innovator of mass production, but just before 1800, Eli Whitney, of cotton gin fame, found a way to manufacture muskets by machine, producing interchangeable parts.

Bix Beiderbecke, the renowned jazz musician, did not play the trumpet. His instrument was the cornet.

Lucrezia Borgia was not the wicked murderess she is reputed to have been. Her major fault, according to Bergen Evans, was "an insipid, almost bovine, good nature."

Contrary to much popular usage, hoi polloi does not refer to the elite; rather, it means the common people.

Natural gas, the kind used for heating and cooking in the home, is odorless. Odiferous additives are put in to give the gas a recognizable smell as a measure to alert people to gas leaks.

Muhammad Ali did not win the heavyweight gold medal at the 1960 Rome Olympics. His gold in 1960 was in the light heavyweight category. The heavyweight gold went to Franco De Piccoli of Italy.

Sacrilegious means violating or profaning anything sacred. In spite of its frequent mispronunciation, the word is not related to *religion* or *religious*.

PAINTED INTO A CORNER

A staple of comedy is the painter who, after refinishing a floor, turns to survey his work only to discover that he has painted himself into a corner, leaving himself no way out. We laugh because we find it hard to believe that anyone could really be that inept and unaware of the consequences of his or her actions. And, in truth, despite the old joke, it most probably never actually happens.

Don't you believe it. As in this analogous occurrence.

In his *Book of Heroic Failures*, Stephen Pile relates a story about the residents of Bennett Court—a retirement home in Otley, England—who, in 1979, decided their residence was too exposed to casual passersby and thus was sorely in need of increased privacy. They met in committee and issued a petition to the town requesting that a fence be erected around their property to provide the seclusion they felt they needed.

The town fathers agreed to their request and in a short time several workers of the council showed up in their truck with all the materials needed to construct such an enclosure. And construct they did, with exemplary speed and efficiency. Within a week they had erected a fence 100 yards long and 3.5 feet high.

On its completion, the workmen were pleased with the look of what they had produced but, on closer examination, were appalled to discover that although their fence was a model of craftsmanship, they had not left an opening to allow their truck to be removed. So the following day they returned to take down enough of the fence to create an exit for their vehicle.

A resident of the home, who had watched the fence being completed, was reported to have observed, "It was like watching a Laurel and Hardy film. Some of us wondered about the lorry, but we didn't want to interfere."

FRENCH FRIES

{ One might imagine that French fries, the snack choice of many high school kids, were conceived of in France. **Don't you believe it.** }

The dish seems more likely to have originated in Belgium. Belgian historians trace fried potatoes in their country to the 1680s, when they were often consumed as a winter substitute for the regional small fried fish ordinarily served as a side dish, the fish becoming unavailable as the rivers froze. "Frites" are the national snack of Belgium, sold widely on the street from fry shacks called *fritures* or *freitkots*.

Although most Americans ascribe the food to France, the French generally recognize it as originating in Belgium. The dish is a favorite around the world, but only in the United States and Canada is it known as "French fries." In the UK and the Common-wealth countries, fried potatoes are called "chips"; in most of the rest of Europe, they are known as "pommes frites" or just "frites."

But whence the "French" component of the name? No one knows for certain, but theories abound. Some speculate it was brought back by World War I doughboys who had tasted them in French-speaking Belgium. Others propose that the name is a misinterpretation of "franged" (meaning "broken") fries. Still others root the name in the menu of a Jefferson White House dinner, which included "potatoes served in the French manner" (meaning deep-fat fried). And still others link it to the cooking term "french," meaning cut into thin strips; however, the *Oxford English Dictionary* dates this term to about one hundred years after the advent of the fries, thus this use of the term "French" is based on the name of the dish, rather than the other way around.

Some argue that the word should be "french," with a small "f," since it relates to a process and not a nationality. In any case, with the worldwide incursion of American fast-food chains, the spuds are now increasingly called "American fries."

THUMBS-UP

> The "thumbs-up" sign for approval, popularized by movie critics Siskel and Ebert, among others, originated in the gladiatorial games in the Roman Colosseum, where thumbs-up indicated the gladiator should be allowed to live; thumbs-down meant the gladiator was to be killed.
> **Don't you believe it.**

The thumbs-up ritual has been repeated in several cinematic Roman spectacles when the victorious combatant waits for the judgment of the crowd. But it is not historically accurate.

As a matter of fact, using a thumbs-up as a sign of approbation is a twentieth-century interpretation, totally opposite to its meaning in ancient Rome. When judging a gladiator, thumbs-up originally meant "send him to the gods"—that is, kill him. Thumbs-down signified dropping the sword—that is, let him live.

In *The Macmillan Book of Proverbs, Maxims, & Famous Phrases*, editor Burton Stevenson cites a number of Roman authors—such as Horace, Juvenal, and Prudentius—and several more contemporary writers who are in agreement that the thumbs-up was the signal to end the gladiator's life, and thumbs-down spared it. The *Oxford English Dictionary* concurs. Nor has the current interpretation of this gesture been long-standing. According to Bergen Evans' *Dictionary of Quotations*, "Throughout the nineteenth century, 'thumbs up' was in England an expression of disapprobation."

When and why the reversal in meaning? No one knows for sure, but Ashley Montagu, in his *The Prevalence of Nonsense*, attributes the origination of the switch to an 1873 canvas by French painter Jean Léon Gérôme, in which the artist portrays spectators in the Colosseum holding their thumbs down, demanding the death of a gladiator. The painting is extremely graphic and has become well known through several reproductions.

"SAVE OUR SHIP"

{ "SOS" is universally used as a signal for a maritime emergency. It is generally thought to mean "Save Our Ship."
Don't you believe it. }

Contrary to popular belief, the distress signal "SOS" does not mean "Save Our Ship"—nor does it mean "Save Our Souls" or "Send Out Succor" or any other three-word phrase. It is simply a Morse message signifying that a ship is in trouble and requesting other stations to immediately cease all telegraphic traffic and to answer the distress call. This code was never meant to be translated into letters. This Morse signal, three dots followed by three dashes followed by three dots ($\cdot\cdot\cdot$ — — — $\cdot\cdot\cdot$), was adopted because it was clear and unlikely to be confused with any other signals.

Before radio communication became possible, ships at sea were isolated and incapable of summoning help if help was needed. At the close of the nineteenth century, wireless telegraphy became possible, but early radio transmitters could not send full-audio signals. So, stations adopted the Morse code of dots and dashes to send messages. Abbreviated signals were much more likely to be accommodated.

In January 1904, "CQD" had been suggested as the signal for requesting assistance, but at a meeting of the International Radiotelegraphic Convention in November 1906, the German government's *Notzeichen*—the three-dot-three-dash-three-dot signal—was standardized as a distress call, to become effective on July 1, 1908.

The above phrases, as well as others used as mnemonic devices to help remember a Morse code, came into being well past the adoption of the international distress signal. In International Morse Code, three dots is an "S" and three dashes is an "O," so the signal has become interpreted as the acronym "SOS."

WASHINGTON'S WOODEN TEETH

{
George Washington's dour expression in several of his paintings is said to result from the discomfort of ill-fitting false teeth made of wood.
Don't you believe it.
}

We know that Washington suffered dental problems for most of his life. His diaries make frequent reference to dental pain. His papers reveal that from the age of twenty-four he lost, on average, one tooth a year, and by the time he was elected president he had only two of his own teeth left. It is estimated that when he famously crossed the Delaware, he had only nine teeth remaining, and at Valley Forge he was down to seven, which left him fewer to chatter in that frigid winter.

Over his lifetime, Washington consulted with several different dentists. But only one was successful in making teeth for him that were at least minimally comfortable—the prominent Dr. John Greenwood of New York City, who later became known as the "father of modern dentistry." Dr. Greenwood used various materials to produce several sets of dentures for Washington; his favorite was fashioned from hand-carved hippopotamus ivory and gold. The upper and lower plates were hinged with springs that held them in position when they were opened; Washington had to bite down in order to keep his mouth closed. If he relaxed his jaw, his mouth would uncontrollably pop open by itself.

Later, Washington's dentures were donated to the University of Maryland Dental School. One set is on permanent display at the National Museum of Dentistry in Baltimore. Interestingly, another, which had been loaned to the Smithsonian to be exhibited in its bicentennial display in 1976, was stolen and has not been seen since.

Washington's false teeth gave him lifelong problems, but none were made of wood.

VOYAGE OF THE PILGRIMS

{
The first permanent New England settlement was established by the Pilgrims, who left England for the New World on a boat called the *Mayflower*.
Don't you believe it.
}

The above statement is essentially true but not quite that straightforward. The Pilgrims' journey did not originate in England but rather in Leyden, Holland, to which they had migrated a dozen years earlier. The Pilgrims were a Separatist faction of the Puritans—"Separatist" because they chose to leave the Church of England, objecting to its secular trappings; other Puritan dissenters opted to remain in the Church and "purify" it from within.

Although the Pilgrims had found religious freedom in Holland, they gradually became alarmed with the increasing loss of their English identity as their children began to adopt Dutch customs and the Dutch language. To better preserve their cultural heritage, they decided to move their entire congregation to the New World, where they could still be unequivocally English but maintain their own manner of church detached from the central authority.

A group of thirty-five Pilgrims departed Holland in July 1620 on a boat called the *Speedwell*. They stopped at Southampton to load supplies and meet up with more pilgrims, other emigrés, and another vessel, the *Mayflower*. The two boats set sail for the colonies in August. But the *Speedwell* proved unseaworthy, and its passengers were transferred to the *Mayflower*, which finally left England on September 6, the Pilgrims constituting about half the number on board.

In November, the voyagers made landfall at Cape Cod.

Thus, while the Pilgrims did indeed arrive on the *Mayflower*, it was not the boat they had originally boarded to depart to the New World from Europe.

"ONE SMALL STEP FOR MAN"

{
The first spoken message to Earth from the moon may have been misunderstood.
You can believe it.
}

Astronaut Neil Armstrong was assured a place in history when he became the first person to set foot on the moon's surface, stepping off the Lunar Excursion Module on July 20, 1969. As commander of the Apollo 11 mission, Armstrong came prepared with a message meant to commemorate this momentous day. His communiqué heard back on Earth has become part of history, surely one of the most memorable phrases ever uttered: "That's one small step for man, one giant leap for mankind."

But what was heard on Earth was not exactly the text Armstrong had rehearsed.

In celebration of the historic event, Armstrong's prepared message began, "That's one small step for *a* man . . ." And here is where the controversy enters: Did Armstrong simply forget the word "a" in the exhilaration of the moment? Or did the word get lost in the comparatively rudimentary sound equipment available at the time? NASA claimed a glitch in transmission obscured the word, making it difficult to hear. But a number of observers, listening carefully, found no gap between "step for" and "man." Several news media, including the *New York Times*, reported what they had heard, his words uttered without the "a," thus changing the intended meaning of the first-ever audio communication from the moon to the Earth.

Several sound experts have analyzed the tapes electronically, but their findings are inconclusive. Some hear the word "a," others do not. In any case, the scientific and cultural significance of Armstrong's achievement overshadows what may have been a verbal slip; the line, regardless of its intended wording, has become legendary.

NATHAN HALE

Nathan Hale, remembered as a patriot and America's first spy, was executed by the British on September 22, 1776. On that day, Hale told his executioners, "I regret that I have but one life to give for my country." A glorious statement created in the passion of the moment.

Don't you believe it.

Hale's mission is well known. The Colonials had retreated from New York City under British attack. Hale, an officer in the Continental Army, volunteered to infiltrate behind British lines to observe the enemy's troop strength, but he was captured and sentenced to be hanged. His last moments were witnessed by a British Captain, John Montresor, and described to Captain William Hull, who reported, in his memoirs, that just before being hanged, Hale uttered those memorable words.

A noble sentiment, but not an original one.

In *Cato*, a popular 1713 drama by Joseph Addison, the playwright states, in act 4, "What pity is it that we can die but once to serve our country." Some historians have speculated that Hale's last words were intended not as a farewell speech but rather as a quote from Addison's play.

But this sentiment traces back well before the eighteenth century. In Book XV of the *Iliad*, Homer wrote: "A glorious death is his who for his country falls." And in Book III of the *Odes*, Horace wrote, "It is sweet and glorious to die for one's country."

A contrarian view was expressed by Ernest Hemingway in *Notes on the Next War*. With characteristic cynicism, Hemingway said, "They wrote in the old days that it is sweet and fitting to die for one's country. But in modern war there is nothing sweet nor fitting in your dying. You will die like a dog for no good reason."

Nonetheless, Hale has made it into history. In 1985, he was officially named Connecticut's state hero.

CONGRESSIONAL MEDAL OF HONOR

{
The Congressional Medal of Honor is the name of the highest award to a member of the United States armed forces for conspicuous valor in military action against an enemy.
Don't you believe it.
}

Technically, there is no such award as the "Congressional Medal of Honor." Its proper name, since its inception in July 1862 during the Civil War, is simply "Medal of Honor." The word "Congressional" is sometimes informally prefixed because the president awards it "in the name of the Congress."

To compound the confusion, the organization dedicated to memorializing the medal and its recipients is called, oddly enough, the Congressional Medal of Honor Society—the appellation supplied by Congress in 1958. Here, the word "Congressional" is apparently meant to refer to the origins of the society, not to the official designation of the medal.

Actually, there are three versions of the medal, one for each branch of the military—the army, the navy, and the air force. The Navy Medal is also awarded to U.S. Marines, inasmuch as the Marine Corps is organized as a branch of the navy, and also to members of the Coast Guard.

Along with the medal, recipients are entitled to several benefits, among them an enhanced retirement pension, commissary and exchange privileges for the awardee and family, and eligibility of his or her children for admission to a U.S. military academy independent of quota requirements.

Among the more than 3,400 Medals of Honor ever awarded, only one has been received by a woman—Dr. Mary Edwards Walker, a Civil War surgeon. In 1917, on review of combat awards, her medal was nullified, along with several others, but after reconsideration it was reinstated in 1977 by President Carter.

THE EDSEL

The products of American manufacture have historically been pretty darn good. But now and then, when
a big company makes a mistake, the result can be a
prodigious embarrassment, one that is widely publi-
cized and long remembered.
You can believe it.

But few failures match that of the Ford Company's Edsel, put
on the market late in 1957. From its debut, the car was plagued by
poor performance: there were reports of side doors that wouldn't
close and trunk doors that wouldn't open, of horns that stuck and
hubcaps that didn't, of batteries that died and paint that peeled.
The hood ornament would fly off at high speed, and the taillights,
as they were configured, appeared to point in the direction opposite of the intended turn.

In attempting innovation, its designers placed the automatic
transmission control on the steering wheel hub, where drivers
inadvertently shifted gears when intending to honk the horn.
Quipsters at the time redefined the D, L, and R codes to mean
drag, leap, and race, rather than drive, low, and reverse. It was a
classic example of Murphy's Law: Anything that could go wrong
did go wrong, and the parent company suffered the wrongs.

From the start, the car was a marketing disaster. With a grille
that was described by some as a toilet seat, by others as a horse
collar, the Edsel was a large, lavish automobile reaching the market
when the public's taste was turning toward economy models. *Time*
magazine observed, "It was a classic case of the wrong car for the
wrong market at the wrong time."

Unpopular when first put on the market, its reputation
decreased from there. One waggish business writer observed that,
in his experience, he knew of only one instance of an Edsel ever
being stolen.

GREAT DANE

> The English foxhound is from England, the Russian wolfhound is from Russia, the French bulldog is from France, the Siberian husky is from Siberia, and, of course, the dog known as the Great Dane is from Denmark.
>
> **Don't you believe it.**

As best as the experts can determine, the Great Dane is a breed that developed in Germany, where, since 1880, it has been recognized as the country's national dog. Classified as a hound, in most non-English-speaking countries it is called the Deutsche Dogge, or German mastiff; among dog fanciers everywhere, it is affectionately known as "the Apollo of dogs."

Registered as a recognized breed, the Great Dane was originally developed to hunt boar, guard castles and estates, and pull carts. Imposing in stature, the adult male stands about 30 to 32 inches high at the shoulder and weighs approximately 140 to 175 pounds. Though distinguished by its large size and courageous disposition, the Great Dane is a perfect family dog—loyal, social, affectionate, playful, and patient around children. Said to have a natural suspicion of strangers, the Great Dane is also a good watchdog and protector.

The breed originated from dogs of the mastiff family—likely the English mastiff—but is believed to have some Irish wolfhound blood in its lineage.

But where did the name for this breed originate? The French naturalist Georges-Louis Leclerc, Comte de Buffon, in his 1749 *Histoire Naturelle*—using the breed as an example of evolution—coined the name "*le Grand Danois*," which in English translates as "Great Dane."

Known for its elegant athleticism and its affable personality, its power and its congenial nature, the Great Dane has earned a widespread reputation as "the gentle giant."

SHIPBOARD MARRIAGES

{
The captain of a ship is empowered to perform marriages on his or her ship while at sea.
Don't you believe it.
}

This is one of the most widespread, deeply ingrained myths. In truth, the captain of a ship—whether pleasure, commercial, or military—has no authority to marry people unless he or she is also a recognized religious leader (e.g., a minister, priest, rabbi) or a judge, justice of the peace, county clerk, or other designated public official.

The misbelief is so pervasive that the U.S. Navy has seen fit to formally codify its prohibition. Cecil Adams, in *The Straight Dope*, quotes the *Code of Federal Regulations* (32 CFR 700.716) which explicitly disallows the commanding officer from performing or permitting the performance of a marriage ceremony "on board his ship or aircraft" when the craft is outside U.S. territory, except if the marriage is "in accordance with local laws" and there is a U.S. diplomatic or consular official in attendance. Adams also cites the official logbook of the British Mercantile Marine Office, which similarly instructs their senior officers that marriages performed aboard ship by the captain are not legal.

The legend likely originated from the venerable belief that, while at sea, the captain is the ultimate authority on his or her ship and can therefore exercise any rite in lieu of the official usually ordained to perform it. True, the captain of a ship has wide discretionary powers in most situations that can arise out of port; but limitations do exist, among them the proscription of authority to conduct a marriage.

One authority has explained it simply: A captain can perform a marriage on board his or her ship only if he or she is authorized to perform marriages on land.

No-hitters

A no-hit game is the dream of every baseball pitcher. But such performances are rare, even by the best pitchers. In the archives of the major leagues, only 257 no-hit games are documented as of the end of 2008. Pitcher Nolan Ryan, known as the King of No-hitters, holds the record with seven such games, the first with the California Angels on May 15, 1973, and the last with the Texas Rangers on May 1, 1991. But have two opposing pitchers ever concurrently thrown a no-hit game?

You can believe it.

In the annals, there was an historic game played in Chicago on May 2, 1917, in which both pitchers threw nine innings of no-hit ball. In this double no-hitter pitching duel, James "Hippo" Vaughn held the mound for the Chicago Cubs and Fred Toney threw for the Cincinnati Reds. With the score tied at 0–0 at the end of the ninth inning, the game went into extra innings. So within the bounds of a standard baseball game, both pitchers would have racked up no-hitters.

But the game continued, and in the top of the tenth, with one out, Vaughn allowed Reds shortstop Larry Kopf a one-base hit. Then Chicago outfielder Cy Williams dropped a fly ball, putting runners on second and third. Next up was Jim Thorpe, the Olympic star turned Cincinnati outfielder, who hit an easy grounder to the mound. Vaughn threw to the plate trying to catch Kopf coming home, but the ball got away from catcher Art Wilson and Kopf scored, giving Cincinnati its only run. In the bottom of the inning, Toney retired all three Chicago batters and Cincinnati won the game, 1–0.

It was a memorable experience for the spectators, who witnessed an event not likely to be repeated soon.

MATADOR'S RED CAPE

> When the bullfighter confronts the bull in the corrida, he entices it with a red cape because the color red enrages the animal to the point of attack.
> **Don't you believe it.**

Yes, the cape used by matadors when they challenge *el toro* is red, and the bull does attack it, but not because of its color. What attracts the bull is the movement of the cape, varied and seductive, no doubt enhanced by its brightness and by the shouting of the boisterous crowd. The balletic maneuvers of the matador, matched with the somewhat unpredictable responses of the bull, make for a grand pas de deux on the sand of the arena.

In fact, bullfighters become renowned for their adept handling of the *capa* that causes the bull to charge. In some cases, a particular flourish of the cape is so associated with a particular matador that the pass is named after the one who introduced it. For example, the graceful *chicuelina*—a dramatic move in which the matador directs the bull's path with his arms while simultaneously turning in the opposite direction—is named for its originator, the renowned Manuel Jiménez Moreno, known affectionately by corrida aficionados as Chicuelo.

Red historically *is* the color of the torero's cape, although at the beginning of a match the matador's assistants frequently trouble the bull with cloaks of yellow and magenta, goading him into activity. But the conventional red mantle has its own significance, both for its brilliant color (more for the fans than the bull) and for the fact that it will not show blood should the torero suffer an injury by the bull.

So the red cape remains an integral element in the bullfight, even though the bull, like many other animals, is color-blind.

CATGUT

Catgut is used for of the strings of harps, violins, and other musical instruments, tennis rackets, and archery bows. It is also used for surgical sutures and fishing lines. But does it really come from the innards of a cat?

Don't you believe it.

Catgut is a tough cordlike material that is made from the intestines of several animals, most frequently sheep, but also goats and occasionally horses or donkeys. To prepare the material for use, the intestines are washed, cut into strips, and scraped clean of fat, membrane, and muscle tissue. The materials are then left to soak for several hours in an alkaline solution, following which they are drawn out on stretchers, sorted by size, and twisted into cords of different thickness depending on their intended use.

Catgut has been used for musical instrument strings for several centuries; the preferred variety is manufactured in Italy. The surgical use is of more recent vintage, replacing hemp and silk ligatures, which frequently cause inflammation because the body cannot absorb them. Surgical catgut, which is more practical in medical applications because it is absorbable, is prepared by several methods, including heat and chemical sterilization.

But where did the term originate? The origins are obscure, possibly from confusion of two meanings of *kit*, both a small violin and a small cat, thus *kitgut* (meaning "violin string") may have been misinterpreted as *catgut*. Or the "cat" component may possibly come from a shortening of the word *cattle*, originally defined as any domesticated animal.

In either case, feline fanciers will be relieved to learn that, whatever other indignities our pets may suffer, there is no cat in catgut.

SLAVERY IN THE NORTH

{ Slavery in the American colonies was a Southern phenomenon, virtually unknown in the North. So say most school textbooks.
Don't you believe it. }

Although textbooks discuss slavery as a way of life and an economic necessity in the American South, by and large these books downplay its presence in the North, where it existed as well—at least until the close of the Revolutionary War. In the north, slaves were mostly house servants; in the south, they worked the farms and plantations, growing tobacco, rice, and cotton primarily after 1800.

All thirteen British colonies, to varying degrees, participated in slavery. It is not widely known that the first colony to legalize slavery—in 1641—was not a southern territory, but rather Massachusetts, where slaves worked the extensive tobacco fields. The second slave state was Connecticut, as of 1650. Not until eleven years later did the first southern colony recognize slavery by statute—Virginia, in 1661. Slavery was approved in New York and New Jersey in 1664 and in Pennsylvania in 1700.

It should be noted that George Washington was a slaveholder, as was Thomas Jefferson, who owned almost two hundred slaves at the same time he championed the right to "Life, Liberty, and the Pursuit of Happiness." Even Patrick Henry, remembered for his "Give me liberty or give me death" speech, made his fortune from the toil of the dozens of slaves he owned. Both Jefferson and Henry spoke out against slavery but nonetheless profited from its presence

In 1777, Vermont became the first colony to abolish slavery. The last colony to do so in the North was New Jersey, in 1804, although the laws of that state grandfathered slaves over a certain age into a category not dissimilar to their previous status.

HANDSHAKE

{
The handshake is a polite courtesy, an expression of friendship and sociability, a gesture of mutual affability.
Don't you believe it.
}

Nowadays, the handshake may be seen as such a gesture, but its origins suggest quite the opposite. In more hostile times, when men routinely carried weapons for self-protection, the handshake had a more practical purpose. Upon encountering a stranger, if no threat was contemplated, one might indicate his peaceful intent by showing an empty weapon hand. Nonetheless, a weapon might still be within reach, so tranquillity was enhanced by each grasping the hand of the other to immobilize it.

From this act of mutual self-defense developed the ritual handshake as a form of greeting or an affirmation of mutual understanding that would seem to suggest honesty, toleration, and equality.

Gradually, the handshake took on additional properties, both in social and political interaction and in business dealings; at one time, a handshake signaled a binding agreement that pledged one's good faith and integrity. In more recent times, however, the trust value of the handshake has been considerably downgraded, and it is now little more than a social custom or an insignificant business formality.

In some circumstances, a handshake serves as a recognition device by members of a secret society or other select in-group who identify themselves to other initiates by exercising some variant form of this gesture. One particularly simple modification is the left-handed handshake adopted by the Boy Scouts and Girl Scouts. Another variation is the multistep "power hand-shake" or "dap." Other current variations of the handshake are the "high-five" hand slap and the knuckle-to-knuckle "fist bump" or "pound."

THE COMMON COLD

"Put on your scarf. Otherwise you'll catch a cold."
Who among us has not heard that caution from one
of our parents or from a well-meaning friend? The
implication being that we are less likely to be stricken
with a common cold if we protect ourselves from
chilly weather. It's familiar folk knowledge. But is it
valid?
Don't you believe it.

Even though it is generally accepted as fact, cold or damp air
will not, in itself, bring on a cold. A cold is a respiratory infection
caused not by inclement weather but by a rhinovirus, one that
usually enters the body through the nose. We do know that the
virus is more active at low rather than at high temperatures, and
that colds are more common in the winter months than in June
and July, but the weather of the season is not the culprit.

In winter, people tend to spend more time indoors, are more
likely to be in closer proximity and in more frequent contact with
other peoples' germs, and are breathing air that is refreshed less
often. Also, schools are in operation at this time of the year, and
no setting provides a more fertile breeding ground for transmit-
table viruses than the shared environment of such group settings.
Children also seem to catch colds more often after a visit to a
doctor's office.

Given that the phenomenology of the cold is so well known
to science, why is there no vaccine for it? Primarily because there
are hundreds of different rhinoviruses, only some of which have
been identified. And without clearly knowing the pathogen, drug
companies have not directed much research toward developing
an antibiotic. Besides, there is too much profit in selling antihis-
tamines and other over-the-counter remedies for drug manufac-
turers to actively pursue a vaccine for the common cold.

PAUL REVERE'S RIDE

{ Paul Revere almost single-handedly saved the American Revolution by alerting the militias at Lexington and Concord that British troops were approaching.
Don't you believe it. }

It's a well-known tale, but far from factual. In truth, Revere played only a minor role in the American Revolution and was barely even known by his countrymen until Henry Wadsworth Longfellow, distorting historical fact, wrote the famous poem lauding Revere's "midnight ride."

The true events have Dr. Joseph Warren of Boston learning that a British contingent was being dispatched to capture John Hancock and John Adams and to seize a cache of weapons stored at Concord. Revolutionary leaders Adams and Hancock, if caught, would likely be hanged. They had to be forewarned, and Warren sent two riders—Paul Revere and Richard Dawes—to alert them. The riders were dispatched by separate routes to increase the likelihood of one getting through successfully.

Revere and Dawes independently reached Lexington and met with Adams and Hancock, then took off for Concord, accompanied by a third activist, Dr. William Prescott. The three were intercepted by an enemy patrol outside Lexington, but Prescott was able to escape and make it to Concord. Dawes soon followed, and only Revere was prevented from going farther—a circumstance not mentioned by Longfellow.

Nor were the riders the only ones to mobilize the local militias. The colonists had already organized a warning system, and several patriots spread the alarm that mustered the colonial forces.

Nonetheless, Longfellow's version of American history is widely and uncritically accepted; even, heaven help us, by some historians and writers of history textbooks.

ANDORRA'S WAR WITH GERMANY

{
Hostilities of World War I ended, for all parties, when the Treaty of Versailles was signed in the Hall of Mirrors at the Palace of Versailles on June 28, 1919. **Don't you believe it.**
}

Strange as it may seem, one European country did not officially end its participation in World War I against Germany until 1958. The country was small, certainly not a power in European affairs. Its name was Andorra—technically the Principality of Andorra—an independent republic of less than two hundred square miles located in the eastern Pyrenees Mountains between France and Spain.

Since 1812, when Andorra, along with Catalonia, was annexed by France, it has been under the control of the French nation. During World War I, through its ties with France, Andorra was nominally aligned with the Allies in opposition to the Central Powers. Having virtually no armed forces, the country did not noticeably engage in any military actions of the Great War, but it was included, nonetheless, in the roster of combatant nations.

Slight in both size and influence, Andorra was simply overlooked when the Treaty of Versailles was drafted. Thus Andorra was not included in the peace provisions when the Treaty took effect. So oddly enough, on paper, Andorra was still at war with Germany from World War I and throughout World War II, although it was officially a neutral nation in the latter conflict.

In 1958 someone, exactly who is unclear, discovered that Andorra was not signatory to the Versailles Treaty and was thus legally still in the status of war with Germany. On September 24, 1958, Andorra declared peace with Germany and the state of war between them ceased that day after forty-four years.

CHRISTIAN MARTYRS IN THE COLOSSEUM

{
The Colosseum was the place where the troublesome
Christians were fed to lions or other voracious beasts
by the ancient Romans.
Don't you believe it.
}

Hollywood films such as *The Sign of the Cross* and *Quo Vadis* have graphically documented this grisly activity in pseudoreal-istic portrayals of Christians being martyred by frenzied felines to the cheers of Colosseum crowds. But history à la Hollywood has always notoriously preferred extravagant spectacle over veracity.

In truth, historical research now suggests that not one Christian suffered such a fate in the Colosseum and that such stories are merely pious legends. Lions did their share of depleting Christian ranks in Rome, but not likely at this location. Evidence suggests that it was in the Circus Maximus where Christians were martyred.

No such events at the Colosseum were recorded in contemporary documents or in writings from the Middle Ages. Their first disclosure seems to have come in the sixteenth century, with their occurrence later endorsed by the Church in the mid-eighteenth century, when Pope Benedict XIV declared the Colosseum a sacred site where Christian blood had been spilled in devotion to the Church.

Authorities have attributed these stories to the Church's need to create martyrs for Church reverence and to establish sacred sites for veneration. Several early reports did tell of Christian executions, but their locations had always been identified in vague terms: "in the arena" or "in the stadium," for example. None speci-fied the Colosseum.

Historians now doubt this structure was ever used for mass slayings of Christians. Even the highly respected *New Catholic Encyclopedia* questions the accuracy of such beliefs.

MORE QUICKIES

George Pullman did not invent the sleeping car. The first was in use on the Erie Railroad Company at least twenty years before Pullman's appeared in 1864.

The confrontation at Lexington was not the first organized armed resistance of the Revolutionary War, although it was the scene of the first bloodshed. The first armed encounter occurred almost two months earlier at the bridge over the North River in Salem on February 26, 1775.

Art Shell, the legendary lineman of the Oakland/Los Angeles Raiders, was not the first African American head coach in pro football. That distinction belongs to Frederick Douglass "Fritz" Pollard, who, in 1921, was named coach of the Akron (Ohio) Pros, a team in the American Professional Football Association (precursor of the National Football League).

President Lincoln's Emancipation Proclamation didn't end slavery because it applied only to Confederate states, where he had no authority.

Despite his later pronouncements, Ronald Reagan, our fortieth president, was not a lifelong conservative. Originally a liberal Democrat and a union man (he served twice as president of the Screen Actors Guild), he helped found the California branch of Americans for Democratic Action and was a member of the United World Federation. He switched his allegiance to become a staunch conservative Republican in the early 1960s.

Oysters can be safely eaten in months with no "r" in their name. A U.S. government handbook, *Consumer's Guide*, reports that with modern refrigeration and shucking methods, oysters are edible throughout the year. They are admittedly less tasty in the summer months when they are spawning, but not unhealthy. Other shellfish, however, notably mussels, may present a risk in r-less months.

JOHNNY APPLESEED

{
Johnny Appleseed, an eccentric figure in American folklore, is really only a fictitious character of the early American frontier.
Don't you believe it.
}

This is a common misconception. There really was such a person; eccentric, yes, but certainly not fictitious. John Chapman was born in Leominster, Massachusetts on June 26, 1774. Wanting to give his son a career, his father apprenticed him to an orchardist who grew and managed apple trees. Chapman learned well, and at age eighteen, in 1792, he headed west to put his education into practice.

Chapman was a conservationist who was completely comfortable with nature—an itinerant who never had a home but roamed freely among both the colonists and the Native American tribes. By the early 1800s he was a familiar figure along the frontier, dressed in sackcloth and a tin-pot hat, always barefoot, and carrying bags of apple seeds collected from cider mills, which he planted in several parts of western Pennsylvania and what are now the states of Ohio, Illinois, and Indiana.

But his plantings were not random. They were part of a well-planned business venture. He set up nurseries—reputed to total over a hundred thousand square miles—each of which he would put in charge of a local manager and revisit every few years to tend to the trees and collect the earnings. His orchards were planted before these areas were settled, so by the time the inhabitants arrived he had already produced mature trees for sale.

At that time, it should be noted, apples were rarely eaten but were used for making hard cider. Thus, Johnny Appleseed not only brought fresh fruit to the frontier but also supplied the raw material for the alcoholic beverage of choice.

PRESIDENT JAMES BUCHANAN

Common knowledge identifies Harvey Milk as the first openly gay person to be elected to any substantial political office in the United States, when he was successful in his third candidacy for the board of supervisors of San Francisco in 1977.

But several closeted gays have held various government offices since the founding of our country.

You can believe it.

Among the poorest-kept secrets was one involving two Democratic senators from different states who lived together in Washington and served in the 1830s and '40s. The two, often referred to as "the Siamese twins," were the talk of the capitol. One was William Rufus King of Alabama, minister to France from 1844 to 1846, and in 1852 elected vice president under Franklin Pierce. The other was James Buchanan of Pennsylvania, who in 1856 was elected president of the United States.

After King left for France, Buchanan wrote, "I am now 'solitary and alone,' having no companion in the house with me. I have gone a wooing to several gentlemen, but have not succeeded with any of them."

The only lifelong bachelor to serve as president, Buchanan had an orphaned niece who served as his "first lady." Aside from his two terms in the senate, Buchanan also served as a congressman from Pennsylvania from 1821 to 1831, as minister to Russia from 1832 to 1834, as secretary of state under President James Polk from 1845 to 1849, and as minister to Great Britain from 1853 to 1856.

Although no definitive evidence supports this claim, some historians, notably James W. Loewen in his *Lies Across America*, seem assured that Buchanan was our first, and only, homosexual president. Others only grudgingly admit his apparent homosexuality.

JEANNE D'ARC

{
Jeanne d'Arc, Saint Joan, the Maid of Orleans, La Pucelle: each a familiar alias for the French peasant girl we know as Joan of Arc. Joan, the savior of France, came from a small village named Arc.
Don't you believe it.
}

Though used throughout the world, the designation "Joan of Arc" is actually a misnomer, a misguided translation of her name from French to English. The "d'Arc" of her name does not indicate that she was from a place called Arc; no such place in France has ever been identified. Rather, d'Arc was her surname—her father's name was Jacques d'Arc—and she was born in a village called Domrémy in northeast France. Some authorities spell the name without the apostrophe, as Darc. She never attended school and never learned to read or write.

Her exploits against the English in the Hundred Years' War are well known, as is her fate: she was charged with heresy for claiming to hear voices of saints and for wearing men's clothes (a prohibition found in Deuteronomy 22:5). For both of which she was threatened with death by fire. Actually, at her trial, she recanted her "errors" and was sentenced to life imprisonment. But when she was discovered once again in men's garb, she was declared a relapsed heretic and burned at the stake in the marketplace of Rouen on May 30, 1431, at age nineteen.

Twenty-five years after her execution, a Trial of Rehabilitation declared that the earlier trial was invalid and that she had not committed heresy. Almost five hundred years later, in 1920, she was officially recognized as a saint and is now known worldwide.

But if the real-life Jeanne d'Arc is to be acknowledged as Joan *of* Arc, then why do we not recognize Charles *of* Gaulle, Ponce *of* Leon, or Cecil B. *of* Mille?

BIRTHDAY PARADOX

{
Assume you are in a room with twenty-two strangers. Someone offers you an even-money bet that two of those present have the same birthday. It seems like the odds are in your favor.
Don't you believe it.
}

Given that there are 365 days in the year (other than a leap year) it would seem highly unlikely that two of only twenty-three people would be born on the same date (irrespective of year). But, strangely enough, the probability is better than 50 percent (actually 50.7 percent) that two of the twenty-three people in that room have birthdays on the same day of the same month. It is a mathematical oddity but easy to demonstrate. Well known among statisticians, this phenomenon is known as the Birthday Paradox.

How can it be? To see how it works, we must consider the likelihood of those assembled all having *different* birthdays. Mathematically, the number of birthday choices for one person is (365/365 = 1). The probability that a second person will have a different birthday than the first is (365/365 x 364/365); there are 364 days remaining for the second person's birthday. Add a third and the probability of all three having different birth dates can be computed as (365/365 x 364/365 x 363/365 = .992 or 99.2 percent); conversely, the chance that at least two of the three have the same birthday is (100–99.2 = 0.8 percent).

Continuing the process, by adding more people until the probability of all having different birthdays falls below 50 percent, we find that the line is crossed at twenty-three persons. For twenty-two people, the probability of all having different birthdays is 52.4 percent; for 23 people the probability is 49.3 percent.

So, you would best be advised not to take that bet. The odds, oddly enough, are against you.

BABY RUTH CANDY BAR

{
The Baby Ruth candy bar was named for the great
New York Yankee baseball legend.
You can believe it, or not.
}

According to the manufacturer, the Curtiss Candy Company, the Baby Ruth candy bar, first put on sale in 1921, was named as a tribute to Ruth Cleveland, daughter of former president Grover Cleveland. The young Cleveland had been affectionately called "Baby Ruth" when she was the nation's favorite infant. This, the official story circulated by the Curtiss Company, is widely accepted today.

But doubts still remain. If, indeed, the Company had chosen that name without first negotiating a deal with the Babe, would it not be in their interest to float an alternative explanation for its source just in case the rights to the name were ever challenged in court? Further, it does seem curious for the sweet treat to be named after a child, though popular in her time, who had died of diphtheria in 1904, seventeen years before the Baby Ruth bar made its appearance in the marketplace.

Observers also note that, although Curtiss asserted that Babe Ruth was still unknown in the year the candy bar appeared, in fact he had already made a name as an impressive pitcher for the Red Sox in 1919 and was well on his way to becoming a prominent national sports figure after being traded to the New York Yankees in anticipation of the 1920 season. By 1921, Ruth was firmly established as a star outfielder who was frequently featured in newspaper stories.

We may never know who truly inspired the name. But in any case, the Baby Ruth is still a favorite today. It is now a product of the Nestlé Company, and was recently named the official candy bar of Major League Baseball.

What Happened to Eve?

{
We know that Adam was expelled from Eden. What
about Eve? Does the Bible follow her as well?
Don't you believe it.
}

Genesis 3:23 explains that Adam was sent "forth from the
garden of Eden, to till the ground from whence he was taken"
and Genesis 3:24 relates how cherubim and the flaming sword
were "placed at the east of the garden of Eden," to make certain
Adam would not be permitted to reenter paradise. Thus, Adam's
expulsion is recounted in detail and the impossibility of his return
is made clear.

But, what about Eve? Was she expelled, too? Did she accom-
pany Adam when he was cast out? Or did she leave at a later
time? The Bible is silent on Eve's withdrawal from Eden. We
are not told when or how or to where she departed. It is all the
more curious, considering that it was Eve who had spoken with
the serpent and who first ate the forbidden fruit, which she then
enticed Adam to taste. It would seem likely that she, rather than
Adam, would be the prime candidate for expulsion.

But the Bible does not tell us. At least not in conjunction
with its revelation of Adam's fall from grace.

However, it soon becomes apparent that Eve, too, departed
Eden. In Genesis 4 we find that Eve has been with Adam and has
borne him two sons, Cain and Abel. And later Adam and Eve
had another son named Seth, who (Genesis 4:25) God provided
to replace Abel, who had been slain by Cain. But again we are not
told where, when, or if she still resides with Adam.

After that, she disappears totally from the story. She is
referred to later in the New Testament, in 2 Corinthians 11:3 and
in 1 Timothy 2:13, but only in passing.

Thus, what ultimately became of the first woman remains a
mystery.

THE WINDY CITY

{
Chicago is nicknamed "The Windy City" because of the strength of the frequent gusts blowing off Lake Michigan.
Don't you believe it.
}

Although the prevailing winds off the lake are fairly strong, they are not the source of the city's nickname. Historians and social commentators agree that the epithet originally referred, metaphorically, to Chicagoans as braggarts, especially Chicago politicians who, in the nineteenth century, were known for typically "blowing a lot of wind." But the experts disagree as to when the term was first applied.

The most popular myth has the name being coined by Charles Dana, editor of the *New York Sun* at the time New York and Chicago were vying for the honor of hosting the upcoming Columbian Exposition of 1893. Competition between the two cities grew heated, leading Dana to write an editorial arguing that New Yorkers should not listen to the bombastic "nonsensical claims of that Windy City. Its people could not build a World's Fair even if they won it." As it turned out, Chicago did win the bid and its Exposition did prove a notable success.

But the nickname has been traced further back to an earlier newspaper article in the 1860s in Milwaukee's *Daily Sentinel*, and then to a well-publicized rivalry between Cincinnati and Chicago—competitors both in the meatpacking industry, both cities using the nickname "Porkopolis," and in the game of baseball, the Cincinnati Reds in intense rivalry with the Chicago Whites. Later, more informatively, two articles appearing in the *Cincinnati Enquirer* and one in the *Cincinnati Tribune*, dating to 1876, used the "Windy City" designation to imply that Chicago was prone to braggadocio.

BOTTLED WATER

{ Bottled water is said to be healthier than tap water.
Don't you believe it. }

Considering the vast sums spent on advertising and promoting bottled water, one might assume it truly has some health-promoting properties. And in certain parts of the world, where the quality of drinking water is not adequately monitored and controlled, bottled water may indeed be healthier than that which comes out of the tap or out of the ground. But in most places in the Western world, tap water is just as good as the water that arrives in bottles, both in taste and purity.

In July 2003, *Scientific American* ran an article reporting the results of a 1999 study by the Natural Resources Defense Council (NRDC) in which more than one thousand samples of 103 different brands of bottled water were tested over a four-year period. They found that samples of more than one in six brands had "more bacteria than that allowed under microbiological-purity guidelines." And about one in five contained some sort of synthetic organic chemicals, such as industrial compounds or those used in the manufacture of plastics. They further estimated that "25 percent or more of bottled water is just tap water in a bottle—sometimes further treated, sometimes not." Suppliers of bottled water are not even required to include on their labels details identifying the source of the water.

A 2001 World Wildlife Fund (WWF) study generally confirmed the NRDC findings. The *Scientific American* article pointed out that "bottled water is subject to less rigorous standards and less frequent tests for bacteria and chemical contaminants than those required of tap water." To the best of our knowledge, the situation has not altered since.

Relative to which, it should be noted that in the United States tap water is under rigorous control by regulations of the

Environmental Protection Agency; bottled water is overseen by some similar, but less stringent, regulations of the Food and Drug Administration. There is no consistent control over water bottled and imported from other countries, because each country has its own standards, which no doubt differ widely.

But surely bottled water tastes better. At least it does if you're taken in by labels. On a Penn & Teller TV show, the hosts found that in a blind taste test 75 percent of New Yorkers chose city tap water over bottled varieties. But when tap water was assayed in a trendy California restaurant, bottled elegantly with pretentious sounding labels, Los Angeles tasters contended the decanted waters all tasted far better than the same water that came right out of the same faucet.

Bottled water also raises several environmental concerns. Packaging and shipping consumes raw materials and energy, and empty bottles contribute to litter and solid waste in landfills. The manufacturing process likely adds to greenhouse gases and air pollution. And from a health perspective, some authorities point to the potential danger of chemical leakage from plastic containers into the water.

And one last, and not trivial, observation: the out-of-pocket cost. The San Francisco Department of Public Health, in an April 2004 fact sheet, estimated bottled water to be as much as 1,300 times more expensive than tap water. Even with the exorbitant charges for gas at the pump these days, the price of a gallon of bottled water can easily exceed the price of a gallon of gasoline.

All of which helps to explain why the NRDC, WWF, the Sierra Club, and several public and private agencies all advocate the choice of tap water over bottled water.

PI

> One of those perplexities we encountered in high school math was that of pi (π), the Greek letter that stands for the relationship of the circumference of a circle to its diameter. It's an immutable mathematical constant, not susceptible to misinterpretation.
> **Don't you believe it.**

We had learned that the ancient Egyptians had managed a fairly close estimate, off by less than two-tenths of 1 percent, and that by about 150 C.E. the Greek astronomer Ptolemy had refined the value correct to four decimal places, $\pi = 3.1416$. Using today's sophisticated equipment, high-speed supercomputers have expanded the precise value to about a billion places.

However, it is not well known that the state of Indiana almost legislated the value of pi to be equal to 4.

In 1897, a physician and misguided amateur mathematician from Posey County named Dr. Edward J. Goodwin convinced his state representative, one Taylor I. Record, to introduce a bill in the Indiana legislature asserting the equivalence of area in a circle and a square that are of equal perimeter. Although the bill never mentioned pi, the stated relationship would hold only if $\pi = 4$. Goodwin's idea was to copyright his solution and offer it free to Indiana schools, "provided it is accepted and adopted by official action of the Legislature," but to charge all others a royalty for its use.

The bill passed the General Assembly by unanimous vote and was about to be voted on by the Indiana Senate when a visiting Purdue University mathematics professor named C. A. Waldo happened to see the "Pi Bill" and pointed out its foolishness, thereby saving the state of Indiana from eternal embarrassment—not to mention mathematical and engineering disaster.

WELSH RAREBIT OR WELSH RABBIT

{ Welsh Rarebit is preferred over Welsh Rabbit as the
name of that national dish.
Don't you believe it. }

Odd there should be such confusion over the name of an almost universally offered menu item. Especially when the dish is merely some melted cheese draped over a piece of toasted bread, flavored with mustard or a bit of spice, with beer frequently added to the top, and served with pickles, apple slices, steamed broccoli, or some other accoutrement.

Although the Welsh Rarebit version seems to have been gaining popularity in recent years, the proper name based on its origin is Welsh Rabbit.

Where does the rabbit component come from? Therein lies the point of the name, which reflects a condescension with which the English had formerly looked down on the Welsh, their poorer uncivilized neighbors to the west. By this name, the English, with an air of class superiority and national vanity, could point out that the Welsh were so poor they couldn't even afford to put a rabbit on their table, though rabbits ran wild in the British Isles—thus not so subtly suggesting an ethnic slur.

Then how did the name Welsh Rarebit come about? Several possible explanations come to mind. It could have been a defensive ploy by which the Welsh nominally upgraded their cuisine by defining the dish as a rare bit of culinary exotica. Or possibly a softening of English attitudes, attempting to erase a stigma they had long fostered. Or it might have simply been a reinterpretation by a fanciful etymologist. Or it could have originated in the unbridled rhetoric of menu eloquence: After all, while a rabbit dish might justify a $10.00 restaurant bill, a rare bit could easily go for $30.00.

THE PURITANS AND RELIGIOUS FREEDOM

{ The Pilgrims were a group of English Puritans who came to the New World to escape the restrictive practices of the Church of England, desiring to secure their own separatist church and choose their own pastors. The colony they founded at Plymouth, Massachusetts, in 1620, is cited as a model of religious freedom. **Don't you believe it.** }

Regrettably, that was not the case. Although the Pilgrims came here to escape the religious intolerance of their native land, their pious settlement was just as intolerant of other forms of religion as England had been of theirs. As in the Massachusetts Bay Colony, instituted by the Puritan migration a decade later, the governing theocratic hierarchy disallowed other varieties of worship.

What united the Pilgrims of Plymouth and the Puritans of the Massachusetts Bay Colony was their shared belief in individual salvation by grace directly through faith in Christ, free from the bureaucratic supervision of the Anglican Church. As offspring of the Reformation, they dissented from the Anglicans, acknowledging the authority only of the scriptures, rejecting the jurisdiction of the English church, and eschewing the intervening functionaries of the clergy.

Roger Williams, a nonconformist who, in 1638, was driven out of Massachusetts because he disclaimed the alliance of church and state, founded the colony of Rhode Island, the first to offer true political and religious freedom. Later, Anne Hutchinson, also banished from the Bay Colony, found her way to Rhode Island and with Williams was instrumental in establishing a settlement respecting total separation of church and state, a model later incorporated into the U.S. Constitution.

MUSSOLINI'S TRAINS

{
Whatever else may be said about Benito Mussolini (and much has been said), one item has been repeatedly chalked up in his favor: He made the trains run on time.
Don't you believe it.
}

Mussolini, or, as some of us will remember, "Il Duce," was the fascist leader of Italy from the 1920s to World War II. He had become internationally infamous following his conquest of Ethiopia in the mid-1930s, an adventure that alienated him from the Western democracies. He then aligned himself with Hitler, to whom he served more as a puppet than a partner.

Mussolini was known both for his ruthlessness as dictator and for his grandiose public projects. But he was seen in the States as somewhat of a cartoon character whose administration of his country frequently caused more problems than it solved. His leadership belied the cliché about fascist efficiency. But the oft-cited assertion that "he made the trains run on time" suggested that, at least, he was responsible for bringing some order to an otherwise chaotic regime.

However, this claim, though achieving worldwide recognition, seems to have been less than accurate. Bergen Evans, a mythbuster par excellence, recounted his own personal experience with Italian trains: ". . . the trains did *not* run on time. [I] was employed as a courier by the Franco-Belgique Tours Company in the summer of 1930, Mussolini's heyday, when a fascist guard rode on every train, and [I am] willing to make an affidavit to the effect that most Italian trains on which [I] traveled were not on schedule—or near it. There may be thousands who can support this attestation. It's a trifle, but it's worth nailing down."

In 1945, Mussolini was hanged by Italian partisans.

THIRTEENTH AMENDMENT

{
The question of slavery in the United States was solved
when it was abolished by the Thirteenth Amendment
to the Constitution.
Don't you believe it.
}

The Thirteenth Amendment read, "Neither slavery nor involuntary servitude, except as punishment for crime whereof the party shall have been duly convicted, shall exist within the United States, or any place subject to their jurisdiction." The amendment was proposed by the 38th Congress on January 31, 1865, and was adopted on December 18, 1865.

However, the amendment went down hard in the South, where it offended a long-standing social and economic system. Of the twenty-seven of thirty-six existing states that voted to ratify, the last four to vote for acceptance had been aligned with the Confederacy—namely, South Carolina, Alabama, North Carolina, and Georgia.

But even as it was being adopted, nine states had not yet voted to ratify. Oddly enough, the last holdouts were not preponderantly southern states, as might have been expected. Those that ratified after the amendment was adopted were mostly from the North and West. Six of the remaining nine voted in favor by the end of 1870. Thereafter, in February 1901, Delaware voted for ratification (after having rejected the amendment in February 1865). Then, after a lag of seventy-five years, Kentucky became the penultimate state to ratify, doing so on March 18, 1976 (also having rejected it in February 1865).

But it was not until March 16, 1995, that the last state finally accepted the amendment. Having formally rejected the amendment in December 1865, Mississippi finally voted for ratification—130 years after it officially became part of the Constitution.

Some old habits die hard!

CLOTHES MOTHS

{
If you discover moths in your home, closets should be treated immediately to lessen the chance of damage to your garments and other cloth materials. Good advice?

Don't you believe it.
}

Such advice will sell products, but they will not be effective. By the time you see the fluttering wings, the damage has already been done. The truth is that adult moths do no injury to clothes because they do not feed on fabrics; in fact, they don't eat much of anything. But the adult females do produce eggs, about forty to fifty at a time, which hatch into larvae in about four to twenty-one days, and it's the fabric-eating larvae that are responsible for the destruction, often to irreplaceable items.

The larvae are small, whitish caterpillars, about one half-inch long, that dwell in dark, secluded places like closets or attics, where they inhabit the folds of fabric. They do not fly, so they are not seen unless one really searches for them. They destroy clothing, wool carpets, fur, feathers, upholstery, blankets, other fabrics, and occasionally synthetic fibers. They cannot survive on clean material, but they acquire nutrition by feeding on items that are soiled with some animal product, such as food stains, scalp oil, perspiration, or urine; they may also be attracted by residue from soft drinks, beer, tomato juice, and milk.

All of which suggests the need to keep things clean if they are to be stored. Before putting away cloth items, make sure they are well laundered and ironed or brushed before packing them up, tightly wrapped, preferably in an airtight container with a moth repellent.

And, knowing that it is the youngsters doing the damage, try to be more kindly disposed toward the older generation.

STILL MORE QUICKIES

Eunuchs, sans testes, are capable of having an erection and copulating. What they are not capable of is reproducing.

An "I am no longer responsible for the debts of . . ." notice does *not* absolve a person from the obligation to pay the debts of a spouse, separated or otherwise.

Helen Keller was not born blind and deaf. In February 1882, at the age of nineteen months, she was stricken with a severe illness that doctors now believe was either scarlet fever or meningitis. That ailment resulted in her disabilities.

The twenty-first century did not begin with the year 2000, but with 2001. Year 2000 was the last year of the twentieth century.

Powdered glass does no harm to the digestive system. In fact, for some time it was prescribed as a remedy for worms. Ground glass, on the other hand, can lacerate the stomach and intestines and likely cause severe damage.

Mussolini's private guard was not known as the Brown Shirts; more accurately, they were called the Black Shirts.

Women's sexual desire does not cease at menopause. Endurance may be curtailed, but desire does not disappear.

Suds do not a cleanser make. They have sometimes been added to a cleaning product because consumers erroneously believe they contribute to the product's efficacy.

The Marx Brothers' brilliant mirror scene from *Duck Soup*, in which Harpo poses as Groucho's reflection, is not an original. Charlie Chaplin did the same thing first in a 1916 silent film called *The Floorwalker*.

George W. Bush was not the first president to shirk military service. During the Civil War, Grover Cleveland hired a surrogate to take his place in the army.

BUREAUCRACY

{ Bureaucrats are even more thoughtless than people assume them to be.
You can believe it. }

The stories of bureaucratic bungling and of governmental red tape are legion. They are standard fare for newspaper editors and social commentators. Anyone having had any dealings with government agencies has at least a few personal experiences to relate, some generating Kafkaesque pain, some stunned disbelief, but more frequently eliciting raucous laughter. But here is unquestionably the best I've ever heard:

As the story goes, several years ago a sensitive document was circulating through the cubicles of the Pentagon for review by particular officials at a high level of security clearance. A copy was directed to the head of a relevant department, a senior functionary who was cleared at the appropriate level required to examine the document. When the folder reached his aide's desk, the assistant dutifully read it, initialed it, and delivered it to his superior's in-box. But the assistant had not noticed that his security authorization was a level below that required to access the document.

The next day his boss found the packet in his in-box, and when he cracked the folder he was aghast to discover that his assistant had not only opened it but also read the material before passing it on to him. He directed the whole package back to his assistant's desk with the following note attached: "The enclosure was not intended for your eyes. You should not have read this document. You are not cleared at the requisite security level. National security must be maintained at every stratum of command. Therefore, immediately, you must delete your initials . . . and initial the deletion."

Surrender at Yorktown

{
History texts tell us that the surrender of Cornwallis
to George Washington at Yorktown, Virginia, on
October 19, 1781, ended the Revolutionary War.
Don't you believe it.
}

Cornwallis' army of eight thousand troops capitulated, but
George III was not ready to end the hostilities, and fighting
continued for more than a year and a half thereafter. Cornwallis'
army was not the only British military presence in North America;
it was only a part of General Henry Clinton's total force, estimated
to be more than thirty thousand men.

Though Yorktown was a major victory, Washington knew
that the war was not over. He continued to press Congress to
pursue the buildup of American forces and Congress asked the
states to continue recruiting fighting men. But the citizenry was
tiring of the war and of the financial strains it had produced. Some
six months after Yorktown, the British fleet routed French naval
forces that had contributed to the Yorktown victory by blockading
British supply lines. The war continued, American casualties grew,
and the outcome was still in doubt.

But the fact is that the American Revolution was not simply
a confrontation between two countries. The colonial forces were
supported by the French and the war was only a part of an international struggle in which Britain was facing off not only against
France but also Spain and Holland. In addition to the colonies,
British forces were committed in the Mediterranean, in South
Africa, and in India. Britain could not long maintain its multi-
front war.

Finally, on September 3, 1783, the Revolutionary War
ended when a peace treaty was concluded and Britain signaled its
recognition of American independence.

NEW YORK YANKEE PINSTRIPES

It is a widespread belief that the signature pinstripe uniform of the New York Yankees was designed for Babe Ruth, in an attempt to visually slenderize his portly frame.

Don't you believe it.

Pinstripes, of various width and separation, had been around since Ruth was a schoolkid. According to Marc Okkonen, in the *Baseball Almanac*, they first appeared on several baseball uniforms around 1907, probably initially those of the Chicago Cubs and Boston Nationals, in a pattern of fine lines narrowly spaced but barely discernible from a distance.

By 1912 the pinstripes had widened, making them more apparent, thereafter worn by several teams, but most often by the New York Yankees, for whom the pattern has come to represent the team. The Yankee uniform is now probably the most distinctive and recognizable attire in all sports; the design is so emblematic of the team that books about the Yankees are frequently ornamented with a pinstripe dust jacket.

Incidentally, the Yankees were also the first team to prominently display player numbers on the backs of their uniforms. The Cleveland Indians had experimented with the idea in 1916, exhibiting numbers on players' sleeves, but soon abandoned the practice. In 1929, the Yankees made the numbers a permanent part of the uniforms. Large enough to be easily seen from the stands, each player's number represented his position in the batting order. Thus leadoff hitter Earle Combs wore #1, shortstop Mark Koenig #2, Babe Ruth #3, Lou Gehrig #4, and so on. The system caught on, and by 1932 numbers became a part of the uniforms of all major league teams.

As for the Babe's pinstripes—he may not have supplied the impetus for the uniform design, but no one doubted that it served him well.

"MIRACLE ON ICE"

{
Everyone who witnessed the historic victory of the American hockey team over the Soviets at the 1980 Winter Olympics will probably remember that the Americans, coached by Herb Brooks, had swept all competitors on the way to this last spectacular triumph that brought them the gold medal.
Don't you believe it.
}

If that's what we remember, our collective memory has failed us, because that's not what happened. Yes, the American team did achieve a momentous victory over the USSR skaters, but it was not the culmination of a winning streak. The U.S. squad came into the game undefeated, but not as consistent winners. Nor was this the game that decided the gold.

In their opening game against Sweden, it seemed, for a while, that the American team would lose out in their very first showing. But they amazingly scored in the final few seconds to avoid what had appeared to be an imminent loss, and they came away with a 2–2 tie. Though not a win, the ending was a significant morale booster because Americans had a long losing record against Sweden, whom they hadn't beaten since 1960.

They then went on to defeat Czechoslovakia, Norway, Romania, and West Germany, and soon had to face the Soviets. The match seemed lopsided, a squad of college athletes facing off against an undefeated team of seasoned Soviet veterans. But youth had its day, and the Americans carried it, to the surprise of most sportswriters and Olympic observers. The Americans won—the game, but not yet the gold medal. They still had to face Finland in a final match that would determine whether they would win the big prize or no medals at all.

But the Americans had the momentum, and they came from behind to overcome Finland 4–2. The U.S. team took the gold in what will long be revered as the unlikely "miracle on ice."

CYRANO DE BERGERAC

{ Cyrano de Bergerac is a fictional character created by
French playwright Edmond Rostand.
Don't you believe it. }

Savien Cyrano de Bergerac was a real historical figure who
lived in France from 1619 to 1655. As in Rostand's romantic
classic, Cyrano was an accomplished swordsman, a popular poet,
and a writer, and he did have an overly large nose.

He published two plays, *La Mort d'Agrippine* (1654) and *Le
Pedant Joué* (1654). But his most famous works were two stories
in the fantastic voyage tradition, both published posthumously:
Voyage Dans la Lune (1657) and *L'Histoire des États et Empires
du Soleil* (1662). Noted science fiction writer Arthur C. Clarke
has credited Cyrano with first incorporating the idea of rocket
propulsion for space travel. He is also credited with having been
an influence on later authors such as Jonathan Swift and Voltaire.

As in the play, Cyrano's outspokenness and intellectual
honesty earned him many influential enemies. As a satirist and
freethinker, he repeatedly repudiated authority and impugned the
Church. His unreserved criticism of the Church is believed to
have helped prevent his ascendancy in literary circles of the time.

But unlike Rostand's character, who is portrayed as a heart-
broken admirer of his cousin, Roxane, the real Cyrano's best
documented love interest was French musician and poet Charles
Coypeau d'Assoucy, with whom he had a thirteen-year relationship until their tumultuous breakup in 1653, which led to each
later writing satirical texts about the other.

Either in an accident or an attempt on his life—the circumstances are undocumented—Cyrano suffered a debilitating head
injury in 1654 from which he never fully recovered, and he died
in July 1655.

BOSTON TEA PARTY

On December 16, 1773, a group of colonists dressed as Indians boarded a ship anchored in Boston Harbor and tossed chests of British tea overboard as a protest against a tax on tea imposed without their consent. The citizens were objecting to a feared increase in the price of their precious tea. So goes the story, memorialized in American history as the Boston Tea Party. **Don't you believe it.**

The facts tell it somewhat differently. The colonists did not expect an increase in their taxes; quite the opposite. Influential merchants feared for their market dominance in the tea trade.

The Tea Act, designed to save the East India Company from bankruptcy by making its prices more competitive, actually reduced the duty on imported British tea, which then lowered the price to the consumer. But the spectre of competition threatened the brisk commerce in smuggling tea from Holland by American traders, notable among them John Hancock. The expectation of cheap British tea caused the famous incident, not the imposition of a new tax or an anticipated increase in the cost of living.

But the event was strategically misrepresented as a popular demonstration against a repugnant autocracy. In truth, the incident was engineered by American commercial interests, acting to preserve their control of the profitable American tea business.

However, not all colonists applauded the event. Benjamin Franklin felt the East India Company should be reimbursed for the loss of its property. George Washington feared the incident would bring British retaliation. It was, after all, a crime—the wanton destruction of another's property—but became a patriotic landmark.

DUMB THIEF

{
Thieves, given the dangers of their chosen avocation, are exceedingly self-protective.
Don't you believe it.
}

We've all heard stories about the stupidity of some crooks. Like the bank robber whose demand note to the teller was written on the back of an envelope addressed to him. Or, the second-story man whose escape from the fourth floor was literally broken up when he tried shinnying down an unsecured drainpipe leaning against the building. Or, the purse snatcher who tried to get away by jumping on a bus, pulling a gun, and ordering the driver to take him to Cuba.

But my favorite is the account of the robber who was on the prowl one night searching for a likely target of opportunity when he came upon a closed jewelry store apparently ripe for the picking. In the darkened window he spied a virtual cornucopia of expensive-looking baubles, a sight providing a temptation he was unable to resist. Having neglected to bring his tool kit, he needed something he could use to break the window. He looked around, but the street was empty, devoid of litter or even one providential garbage can. With no means of entry available, he was about to pass on this hoard of gems when right behind him he spotted a manhole cover, which provided the implement he needed. He yanked it up and smashed it through the glass.

While filling his pockets with loot, he heard the approaching siren of a police car no doubt summoned by the store's security system. He grabbed as much as he could carry, stuffed his pockets, and turned to run. But he had taken just a few steps when he fell into the open manhole, not only assuring his capture but also breaking a leg in the process.

PANAMA CANAL

{
It is common knowledge that the Panama Canal runs from the Caribbean Sea to the Pacific Ocean, thus east to west or, of course, west to east from the Pacific to the Caribbean.
Don't you believe it.
}

Any geographical atlas will confirm that Central America is bordered on the east by the Caribbean Sea and on the west by the Pacific Ocean. But a close look at a detailed map of that part of the world will reveal that the section of Central America known as the Isthmus of Panama follows a curious route just where the Canal is located. Here, the isthmus runs east and west rather than north and south.

The path of the canal was designed to take advantage of the narrowness of the land bridge and of several artificial lakes that are higher than sea level. The convenient placement of the lakes explains why the peculiar route followed by the canal runs northwest to southeast such that the Pacific end to the west is further east than the Caribbean end and the Caribbean end to the east is further west than the Pacific end. Takes a bit of adjustment to understand, but it is demonstrably true.

It might be more instructive to observe that in this area, on the map, the Caribbean is actually on the north side of the canal and the Pacific on the south. The geography of the canal has perplexed travelers for a long time. It is especially confusing when traversing the canal and discovering the ship is actually heading southeast to go west to the Gulf of Panama, an arm of the Pacific, or, on the opposite route, heading northwest to go east to the city of Colón on the Caribbean Sea.

This simply confirms an observation of cruise ship devotees: World travel can be as perplexing as it is instructive.

HARRY S TRUMAN

Harry S Truman was the thirty-third president of the United States. His accomplishments are well known, but much confusion still exists about his middle initial and the name the middle initial stands for. It may have several meanings.
You can believe it.

Actually, Truman did not have a middle name, only a middle initial, which he once said was his middle name. In his autobiography he wrote, "My Grandfather Truman's name was Anderson Shippe Truman and my Grandfather Young's name was Solomon Young, so I received the S for both of them." This was decided, it seems, because his parents wanted to remain impartial in not honoring one family's lineage over the other. Also, it should be noted that at that time it was not at all an uncommon practice in the South, Missouri included, to assign initials rather than names.

When Truman joked to reporters that the "S" didn't stand for anything, he added that since it was really a name and not an initial, it didn't require a period following. But in the name of the Harry S. Truman Presidential Museum and Library in Independence, as well as in his signature on scores of official documents, the letter *is* followed by a period. The period also appears on the United States Navy aircraft carrier, designated the USS *Harry S. Truman*.

However, the issue is not clearly resolved. His official White House biography, for example, does not use a period, nor does the name of the Harry S Truman National Historic Site (property including the family farmhouse in Grandview, Missouri), while most style manuals do prefer including the period.

So it remains for future researchers to work out the political legacy of the Truman "period" in American history.

THE GETTYSBURG ADDRESS

{ Lincoln wrote his Gettysburg Address on the back of an envelope, or possibly on a piece of wrapping paper, on the train en route to the dedication ceremony for the new cemetery at the Gettysburg battlefield, to be held on November 19, 1863.
Don't you believe it. }

Lincoln may have made some last-minute emendations to his text, but the speech had largely been written several days previous to his boarding the train. The on-the-train story first appeared as an article by Mary Raymond Shipman Andrews in *Scribner's Magazine* in 1906. Titled "The Perfect Tribute," it was published as a short book the following year. Intended merely as a piece of heroic fiction, it somehow became popularized as valid history.

The featured speaker of the ceremony consecrating the interment site was scheduled to be Edward Everett, a renowned orator of proven eloquence. The invitation to Lincoln appears to have been an afterthought, he being formally invited barely two weeks before the event.

It is known that the speech went through several drafts, the earliest begun while Lincoln was still in Washington, days before entraining for Gettysburg; the first of two pages were written on White House stationery clearly headed *Executive Mansion*. Lincoln expert Edward Steers, Jr. has identified five extant copies of various versions with well-established provenance: two are at the Library of Congress, one each at the Illinois State Historical Library and at Cornell University, and the last on display in the Lincoln bedroom at the White House.

Authorities are still not sure which copy was the one read by Lincoln on that dramatic day. But reviewing the evidence, one thing is certain: none was on the back of an envelope.

READING IN DIM LIGHT

{ Reading in dim light does damage to your eyes.
Don't you believe it. }

This is a piece of folklore that has been handed down for generations, among the long list of cautions instilled in children by their parents. But it isn't true. Reading in low illumination does strain and tire the eyes in their attempt to distinguish visual detail, but it doesn't damage them. The discomfort is caused by the eye having to work harder to focus in low light, compounded by the tendency to blink less, leading to dryness of the eye and an unpleasant sensation. It is the eye muscles that bear the strain, not the visual structures of the eye.

But the eye recuperates quickly once the person ends the dimly illuminated task, and the discomfort soon passes. Low-light visual impairment is temporary. The *AARP Bulletin*, for example, quotes a spokesman for the American Academy of Ophthalmology, who asserts, "You are not doing damage to your eyes; your eyes just may feel cramped or strained."

There are research findings suggesting that reading in poor lighting may aggravate a person's existing myopia, but no convincing evidence that it could be causative. Low illumination demands that the pupil be opened wider to admit enough light to see, which some argue may lead to nearsightedness, but this opinion is not widely held. It should be noted, however, that the level of illumination becomes more consequential for people who also suffer other conditions that hinder vision, such as glaucoma, cataracts, or macular degeneration.

The final word is not yet in, but most vision experts do not believe that stressing the eye with low illumination is likely to result in permanent damage. They liken the situation to that of a physical workout, where the resulting tiredness and debility soon pass once the activity is ended.

PLUTO IN THE SOLAR SYSTEM

{
There are nine planets in our solar system; in order of
their distance from the sun: Mercury, Venus, Earth,
Mars, Jupiter, Saturn, Uranus, Neptune, Pluto.
Don't you believe it.
}

There are only eight planets in our solar system. There had
been nine, but in August 2006 the International Astronomical
Union, for the first time, defined the term "planet," and Pluto fell
short of the requirements. Soon thereafter, the IAU created a new
classification of "dwarf planet" and downgraded Pluto to it.

The new definition of planet encompasses three conditions:
First, it must be in orbit around the sun; second, it must have
sufficient gravity to force itself into the shape of a sphere; and
third, it must have "cleared the neighborhood" about its orbit. The
latter simply means that a planet must be the dominant gravita-
tional body in its orbit such that it either captures smaller objects
in its orbit or flings them out of its path. The third is the require-
ment not met by Pluto, whose mass is only 0.07 times that of
other objects in its orbit. By comparison, Earth has a mass factor
of 1.7 million times.

Pluto is now considered a member of a trans-Neptunian
ring around the sun, first observed in 1992, known as the Kuiper
Belt—a vast repository of icy bodies dating from the birth of the
solar system some 4.5 billion years ago.

A mission dubbed "New Horizons," now in progress, is
designed to provide more data about Pluto's characteristics.
Launched in January 2006, the craft will begin making scientific measurements of Pluto in early 2015 and make its closest
approach in July of that year.

But it should be noted that the IAU's decision is not universally accepted. A number of astronomers still argue that Pluto
should maintain its classification as a planet.

WILLIAM TELL

{
William Tell became a national hero of Switzerland, the symbol of Swiss political and individual freedom, when his arrow took an apple off his son's head. **Don't you believe it.**
}

As the story is told, Tell was a peasant from the town of Bürglen in the canton of Uri in the fourteenth century. At the time, the Hapsburg emperors were trying to subjugate Uri. To assert the power of Austria over the cantons, Governor Hermann Gessler had placed a hat atop a pole and ordered all local towns-folk to bow before it as an avowal of submission. Tell did not, for which he was arrested. Known as an expert marksman with the crossbow, he was sentenced to shoot an apple off his son's head. If he didn't comply, both he and his son were to be executed; if he succeeded, he would be released.

On November 18, 1307, Tell split the apple with a single shot, whereupon Gessler asked Tell why he had a second arrow in his quiver. Tell replied that if he had killed his son the second arrow would have found Gessler as well. Tell was rearrested but managed to escape, and some time later killed Gessler.

Tell's defiance of Austrian authority led eventually to rebel-lion and later to the formation of the Old Swiss Confederacy. Tell soon became a heroic figure in Switzerland and his story has become legend. Pure legend, as it turns out, because modern authorities agree it is only a myth. In some Swiss cantons, the story has been deleted from schoolbooks.

In fact, a similar tale appears in the folklore of other nations, notably in German and Norse mythology, and in English and Danish tradition.

Doubtful or not, the tale has been retold in a play by Friedrich von Schiller and an opera by Rossini.

THE ROUGH RIDERS

{ Teddy Roosevelt made a name for himself in the Spanish-American War leading his Rough Riders in a cavalry charge up San Juan Hill in Cuba.
Don't you believe it. }

Roosevelt, known as a fearless if reckless warrior, did indeed distinguish himself in that conflict, but not in the manner usually described. As a lieutenant colonel, he commanded a regiment of cavalry volunteers in a fierce battle against entrenched Spanish forces in July 1898. But his soldiers were not on horseback; they fought on foot, having left their mounts in Florida for lack of transport space. Roosevelt, as commanding officer, was the only one in the saddle.

Later to become the twenty-fifth president of the United States in 1901, Roosevelt had been stationed in Washington as assistant secretary of the navy but had an overwhelming desire to get into the war. He resigned his governmental position and set out to organize his own volunteer cavalry, which he was determined to have a role in the hostilities.

But we now know that his attack, foolhardy though successful, was made not on San Juan Hill but rather on nearby Kettle Hill, a comparatively minor action in the larger battle for San Juan Heights. Nonetheless, his volunteer regiment, advancing in the face of well-manned Spanish rifles, had distinguished itself by performing as well as any of the regular army units in the encounter. Roosevelt's bravery was apparent, but his judgment has been called into question; his regiment suffered heavy casualties.

In deference to the historical record, it should be noted that he did eventually get to the top of San Juan Hill, but only after it had been captured by another regiment.

CENTER OF THE UNIVERSE

> The planets in the universe all revolve around the Earth.
> **Don't you believe it.**

It would seem almost foolish to include this item as a possible presumption in today's world, as virtually no one with even a rudimentary knowledge of science still believes the Earth is the center of our universe. But at one time, almost everyone accepted the Earth as the core force that held the universe together. The Bible taught that man was created in the image of God. And man lived on Earth. So Earth had to be seen as the focal point of the cosmos.

In 1543, the Polish priest and astronomer Nicholas Copernicus released his landmark book *On the Revolutions of the Celestial Spheres*, which argued that the planets, Earth included, revolved around the sun. The idea had been circulating for centuries, having first been theorized by the ancient astronomer Aristarchus of Samos in the third century B.C.E., but was largely ignored until Copernicus published his then-controversial study.

Theologians of the time denied his interpretation of the universe. Even after Galileo had developed the evidence to support it, the Church rejected his proof and sentenced Galileo to house arrest for the remainder of his life, commanding him to renounce his support of the Copernican theory, which the Church declared "false and erroneous." Galileo acquiesced, but, according to Stephen Hawking, "his belief in the independence of science had not been crushed." For most, however, faith conquered science and the majority of people lived in an Earth-centric universe.

While still under house arrest, Galileo produced his second major book, *Two New Sciences*, which offered even more support for Copernicus and angered the Pope still further. But he firmly established the sun as the pivot of the universe, and in doing so set the course for the separation of science and religion.

"THE STAR-SPANGLED BANNER"

{ "The Star-Spangled Banner" was accepted as our national anthem shortly after it was written in September 1814.
Don't you believe it. }

Originally a poem titled "Defense of Fort McHenry," the text was penned by lawyer Francis Scott Key after he watched the bombardment of the Baltimore fort by Royal Navy ships during the War of 1812. Key was detained aboard HMS *Minden* to prevent his revealing details of the plan for the British attack on Baltimore he had heard while on a mission to secure the release of an American physician being held for acts against the Crown.

The bombardment continued for a good part of the night, and when daylight arrived he was delighted to observe the American flag still flying triumphantly over the fort, whereupon he was inspired to record his observations in verse on the back of a scrap of paper from his pocket. The poem was later set to the melody of "The Anacreontic Song," an old British drinking song that had been written in the 1760s by John Stafford Smith.

Gradually attaining popularity in the nineteenth century, Key's song was frequently played during public events, sharing the role with several others, notably "Hail, Columbia" and "My Country 'Tis of Thee." No national anthem had yet been named. Then, in 1889, secretary of the navy Benjamin F. Tracy designated "The Star-Spangled Banner" as the official accompaniment to the raising of the flag. In 1916, president Woodrow Wilson decreed that the tune be played at military and other official events.

And, finally, on March 3, 1931, 117 years after its creation, president Herbert Hoover signed a federal law prescribing "The Star-Spangled Banner" as the official anthem of the United States.

The flag that Key observed on that historic morning is now on display at the National Museum of American History, a branch of the Smithsonian Institution in Washington, D.C.

ELEANOR ROOSEVELT LEAVES THE D.A.R.

{ Eleanor Roosevelt was asked to withdraw her membership from the Daughters of the American Revolution.
Don't you believe it. }

The first lady, though not an active member of the D.A.R., did hold a position on the board of directors.

Rather than being asked to sever her affiliation with the organization, she chose to resign her membership when, in February 1939, the D.A.R. refused to permit a concert by the renowned singer Marian Anderson to be held at Constitution Hall, in Washington, D.C. The D.A.R. owned the hall and had a rule excluding African American artists from performing there. Anderson had already appeared in Carnegie Hall in the early 1930s, and at the White House in the late 1930s, but she was denied the stage that was controlled by the D.A.R.

Mrs. Roosevelt's action generated extensive newspaper coverage deploring the D.A.R.'s decision, and shortly other prominent women followed her out of the organization. The ensuing notoriety prompted Mrs. Roosevelt to arrange a replacement concert for Anderson. The first lady felt it necessary to affirm the broader acceptance of black artists by the country as a whole. The venue chosen was the Lincoln Memorial, and the date was April 9, 1939, Easter Sunday, when Ms. Anderson sang for a crowd of over 75,000 people. Many millions more heard her performance on the radio broadcast of the concert.

Mrs. Roosevelt, by her action, drew attention to the issue of equality for African Americans. The D.A.R.'s unfortunate decision served to publicize the problems inherent in the gulf between the races in the United States and made the entire country confront the growing issue of inequality represented by the racial divide in the nation.

CATHERINE THE GREAT

{ The rumor is that Catherine the Great of Russia died as a result of an unnatural sexual encounter with a horse.
Don't you believe it. }

Catherine was known to be a woman of insatiable sexual appetite, willing to experiment with new and unusual sources of amatory pleasure. The legend tells of her desire to experience a well-endowed stud—four-legged variety. Toward that end, she is said to have had constructed a device to suspend the animal above her. However, the support gave way and Catherine was crushed to death beneath the unfortunate beast. The story is unclear as to whether the accident occurred before, after, or during the encounter.

The source of the tale—characterized by one commentator as a case of "unbridled lust"—is lost to history, but her biographers believe it was concocted to demean her greatness by portraying her as an erotic weirdo who thought of nothing but her own pleasure. She lived, after all, in a period when women were considered biologically inferior to men, whom they were designed to serve, and thus incapable of commanding a nation. Having become empress by wresting power from her husband, she was thought to be an aberration for her time and was dishonestly portrayed as an anomalous creature.

However, she proved to be a savvy monarch who educated her people, installed extensive reforms, and saved Russia from being overrun by more powerful neighbors. Her success elicited derisive tales of contemptible behavior. She simply didn't fit into the stereotype of a woman of her century and had to be discredited.

Actually, Catherine succumbed to natural causes on the night of November 6, 1796, after two days of agonizing coma.

BETSY ROSS

{ Betsy Ross created the first American flag.
Don't you believe it. }

As the story goes, in 1776 Congress ordered George Washington to design a flag for the new country, and he—along with two members of the Continental Congress, George Ross and Robert Morris—visited Betsy Ross at her home at 239 Arch Street in Philadelphia to consult with her on its appearance. It is said that he described the design he had in mind and he left her with a commission to produce it.

But historians have found no Congressional record of such an order or any other documentary evidence from the period confirming that such a commission was granted or that such a flag was ever produced.

Mrs. Ross' claim is based solely on the word of her family members that she had told them this story, a disclosure revealed for the first time by her grandson, William J. Canby, at a meeting of the Historical Society of Pennsylvania in 1870. The only related information unearthed by archival researchers was that Mrs. Ross had at one time been commissioned to produce some ships' pennants for the State Navy Board of Pennsylvania.

Historians now believe the first flag was created not by Betsy Ross but more likely by a member of the Continental Congress, an artist named Francis Hopkinson, who was a signer of the Declaration of Independence. Hopkinson is known to have been a designer of the seal of the state of New Jersey and one of the designers of the Great Seal of the United States.

Although the Ross story has never been confirmed, her home in Philadelphia continues to draw a large number of visitors as a well-known tourist attraction.

There is now even some question as to whether she ever lived at this address.

U.S. EXTREMES

{ What is the easternmost state of the United States? If you think you know . . .
Don't you believe it. }

Try this: What is the westernmost state of the United States? Without much thought, we know it must be either Hawaii or Alaska, both being in or on the Pacific Ocean. As it turns out, it *is* Alaska, several of the Aleutian Islands extending to the 180th longitude, the dividing line between the eastern and western hemispheres.

And what is the northernmost state? That's easy: obviously Alaska, which reaches well above the Arctic Circle, the northern extremity being Point Barrow at 71° 23'N.

And the southernmost state? It's Hawaii, which extends down a full five degrees south of the Florida Keys. Its most southern point is Ka Lae, also known as South Cape, on the island of Hawaii, at 18° 55' N.

But here's the tough one: What is the easternmost state? It would seem obvious that it's Maine. Obvious, perhaps, but it is not necessarily accurate.

Surprisingly, the easternmost state is, at least by one definition, also Alaska. It sounds odd, but it is true, inasmuch as the islands at the tail end of the Aleutian chain stretch past the 180th longitude and are thus technically on the other side of the line that separates the Eastern hemisphere from the Western. The Near Islands and the Rat Islands, both in the Aleutian chain, are all in the east longitudes; the easternmost point being Pochnoi Point on Semisopochnoi Island, at 179° 46' East.

Thus, strangely enough, Alaska is at once the most western, northern, *and* eastern state in the union. A good lesson for our kids: Geography has much to teach us—and it is also a good source of trivia questions that could stump your friends.

HINDENBURG

{
It is widely supposed that all aboard perished when the German lighter-than-air airship *Hindenburg* was destroyed by fire while landing at Lakehurst Naval Air Station in New Jersey on May 6, 1937.
Don't you believe it.
}

The *Hindenburg*, at 804 feet long the largest aircraft ever flown (almost as long as the *Titanic*), was promoted as the forerunner of a new mode of safe, comfortable air transportation likely to replace oceangoing liners.

Named for Paul von Hindenburg, president of Germany from 1925 to 1934, the ship was more than a symbol of German technological mastery; it was a giant propaganda display of Nazi power. It had been in the air at the August opening of the 1936 Olympic Games in Berlin and prominent once again that same year at the September Nazi Party congress in Nuremberg, each of its tail fins conspicuously displaying a large swastika, the symbol of the Nazi Party.

In 1936, its first year of commercial service, it uneventfully completed seventeen transatlantic round trips, ten to New York and seven to Rio. The *Hindenburg* began the 1937 season with a Germany-to-Brazil round trip. On its first transatlantic crossing of the season to North America, it carried thirty-six passengers and a crew of sixty-one. As it began its mooring routine at 7:25 PM that May evening, fire broke out in its rear section, then rapidly spread to engulf the entire craft.

Of the ninety-seven people aboard, sixty-two survived. Killed were thirteen passengers, twenty-two crew members, and one member of the ground crew who didn't move fast enough.

The event had wide and long-lasting ramifications. Along with the *Hindenburg*, the German hope of controlling long-range passenger air service went up in smoke that day.

WOMEN'S SUFFRAGE

{
It is generally accepted that American women did not
have the vote until 1920, with passage of the Nineteenth Constitutional Amendment.
Don't you believe it.
}

This is true for national elections but not for local elections in
a number of states. Before passage of the Nineteenth Amendment,
several parts of the country had already extended full suffrage to
women. The first was the Wyoming territory, which by its constitution in December 1869 gave women the right to vote and to
hold public office. When Wyoming achieved statehood in 1890,
it became the first state to grant women suffrage, calling itself the
"Equality State."

By 1900, women had secured the vote in Utah, Colorado, and
Idaho. After the turn of the century several other states concurred,
and by 1914 all ten of the westernmost states had granted women
suffrage, along with the territory of Alaska. Only New Mexico
demurred.

Oddly enough, New Jersey had (inadvertently?) granted
women voting rights by its first state constitution in 1776. That
document made no gender or race differentiation, requiring only
that the person be an inhabitant and own property of at least
£50 in the state. However, since women rarely owned property
(their menfolk did), only the widowed or the unmarried qualified.
Women's suffrage in New Jersey was rescinded in 1807, limiting
the franchise to white males.

It is interesting to note that the federal women's suffrage
amendment was first introduced in Congress in 1878 but never
came to a vote. Reintroduced in each of the succeeding forty
years, it finally passed Congress in 1919, permitting the several
states to vote on it. After Tennessee ratified it, it was adopted on
August 26, 1920.

LONGEST OVERDUE
LIBRARY BOOK

{
After a certain period, overdue library books are simply written off.
Don't you believe it.
}

But how late was the longest overdue library book?

One well-publicized story that made the world press in February 2006 reported on the return of a copy of *The Punch Library of Humour* that had been borrowed from a library in Rotorua, New Zealand, in 1945, sixty-one years earlier. The book, which turned up among family mementoes in the home of eighty-five-year-old Marie Sushames of that city, had accrued an overdue fee of $6,114. However, the Rotorua library manager offered to waive the penalty in return for being allowed to display the volume as the longest overdue book she had seen in her sixteen years in the library system.

But records show an even more truant volume, this one checked out of the Library of the Medical School of the University of Cincinnati in 1823. The book, titled *Medical Reports on the Effects of Water, Cold & Warm, Remedy in Fever & Febrile Diseases, Whether Applied to the Body or Used Internally*, was written by a Dr. James Currie and printed in London in 1805. After an extended absence, during which the volume was likely forgotten or written off as long lost, it was eventually returned in December 1968 by the borrower's great-grandson.

In the 145 years that the Currie book remained delinquent from the library, it had accumulated a fine estimated to be $2,624. Although it was a serious sum, it was considerably less than that for the *Punch* book, which would suggest that library penalties were significantly less severe in the nineteenth century than in the twentieth.

So the next time your librarian chides you for returning a book a week overdue, mention Currie.

LIZZIE BORDEN

> "*Lizzie Borden took an axe and give her mother forty whacks.*
> *And when she saw what she had done, she gave her father forty-one.*"
> **A familiar children's rhyme, but don't you believe it.**

On August 4, 1892, in Fall River, Massachusetts, Andrew J. Borden and his second wife, Abby, were found hacked to death in their home on Second Street. The local police investigated the gory scene and arrested the Bordens' thirty-three-year-old daughter, Lizzie. Lizzie—one of two people, aside from the victims, known to be on the property at the time of the grisly killings—claimed she was in the backyard barn collecting fishing equipment when the murders occurred. But the grand jury didn't believe her story; they indicted her and Lizzie went to trial before a panel of three judges in June 1893.

What followed is not usually told as part of the story and therefore is not well known. Lizzie was defended by a team of lawyers including George Robinson, a former governor of Massachusetts. As it turned out, the district attorney could produce no hard evidence and his case against Lizzie proved to be entirely circumstantial. The jury responded by returning a verdict of not guilty. And popular opinion also absolved her of the crime. After the trial, she remained in Fall River, moving to a new home and calling herself Lizbeth in place of Lizzie.

But the case had captured the American imagination, producing schoolyard rhymes and other expressions in pop culture. Among them, in the early 1900s, a musical appeared with the distinctly kitschy title, *Lizzie Borden: A Musical Tragedy in Two Axe.*

And, incidentally, examination of the victims revealed that the Bordens had suffered a total of only twenty-nine whacks, not the forty-one of the couplet.

MISSION ACCOMPLISHED

On May 1, 2003, president George W. Bush stood on the deck of the aircraft carrier USS *Abraham Lincoln* and proclaimed the end of major combat operations in Iraq. Behind him hung a giant banner that read MISSION ACCOMPLISHED. The banner heralded impending victory in Iraq.
Don't you believe it.

Critics wanted to know what mission had been accomplished. If the banner was meant to signal the imminent return of all American troops, it was obviously overoptimistic. Sadly the war dragged on, no end in sight.

The proclamation was occasioned by the arrival of a shipload of serviceman returning home from the combat zone. But the whole event was seen as little more than a political stunt.

Press coverage showed Bush arriving on the ship as copilot of a navy jet, no doubt meant to project the image of a decisive, in-charge president while reminding the country of his past as a fighter pilot with the Texas Air National Guard. But critics observed that he could just as well have landed in a helicopter, not posing as a warrior but helping speed the homecoming of the returning soldiers whose ship had to stay longer and farther offshore to accommodate his pretentious arrival, while, incidentally, wasting considerable fuel and other navy resources.

The impropriety of the event was observed by so many commentators that the White House felt it necessary to issue a claim that the banner was the navy's idea. The navy rejected the claim, asserting that the banner came from the White House. The true origin of the banner has never been established.

When Bush left office, in January 2009, the war still dragged on, U.S. troop casualties exceeding 4,200 dead.

PONY EXPRESS

{ The Pony Express had a long history of providing comparatively fast mail service between the center of the country and the West Coast.
Don't you believe it. }

Actually, its history was rather short, lasting only eighteen months, from April 3, 1860, to October 24, 1861.

From St. Joseph, Missouri, to Sacramento, California, a distance of almost two thousand miles, the Pony Express could deliver a letter considerably faster than any other means available. It scheduled ten days' transit time in summer, twelve to sixteen days in winter. The other available options—steamship, stage-coach, or Butterfield Overland Mail—took at least three weeks to cover the same distance.

Adhering to the company motto, "The mail must go through," riders rode day and night in all seasons, each rider in relay covering seventy-five to one hundred miles, changing horses at intermediate stations every ten to fifteen miles.

Starting out, the company advertised for "young, skinny, wiry fellows, not over 18. Must be expert riders. Orphans preferred." Offering wages of $25 per week, the ads frequently included the proviso, "Willing to risk death for the job."

The need for faster communication beyond the Rocky Mountains had grown rapidly as thousands of settlers headed west on the Oregon Trail starting in the 1840s, followed by the 1847 Mormon exodus to Utah and the 1849 gold rush. Mail needed a reliable delivery service and the Pony Express provided it. Of an estimated 35,000 pieces of mail carried, only one sack was ever lost.

But as is the case for nearly all innovations, time caught up with the Pony Express when, on October 26, 1861, a telegraph link was completed between San Francisco and New York City, effectively putting the Pony Express out of business.

LUSITANIA

{
The sinking of the *Lusitania* by a German submarine forced America's entry into the First World War.
Don't you believe it.
}

RMS *Lusitania* was a British ship, not American. It was one of the world's most glamorous ocean liners, designed both for comfort and for speed. In 1908 the *Lusitania* had broken the existing record for a transatlantic crossing. But now the war was battering Europe, and Germany was fighting to control the high seas. It was known at the time that British liners carried munitions as well as passengers, and the German government issued clear warnings that any ship flying the flag of Great Britain would be sunk if sighted in a war zone. And, along with the warning, American travelers were advised to avoid British ocean liners.

On a rainy day in May 1915, such a warning appeared in the morning editions of the city's newspapers as the *Lusitania* pulled out of New York Harbor, embarking on its 202nd Atlantic crossing. The ship carried more than one thousand passengers and a crew of some seven hundred, most of whom were likely unaware of that morning's warning from the German embassy.

On May 7, 1915, the *Lusitania* was sighted off the southern Irish coast. Its captain, rather than pursuing an evasive course, was inexplicably heading directly through the war zone toward Southampton, even though the Admiralty had warned him that enemy submarines were active in the area of the ship's path.

Not surprisingly, the ship was sighted by a U-boat, was torpedoed, and sank. About 1,200 people died.

But this was two years before the United States entered the war. So, although the sinking of the *Lusitania* was not a proximate cause of the United States entering the war, it certainly didn't do much to endear the German nation to Americans.

POPULAR VS. ELECTORAL VOTES

{
In the 2000 presidential election the losing candidate had collected more popular votes than the winning candidate. This was an unusual election outcome. **Don't you believe it.**
}

The disparity between popular and electoral votes has occurred several times in our history.

In the 1824 election, the winner, John Quincy Adams, had accumulated only 105,000 popular votes to Andrew Jackson's 156,000, and 84 electoral to Jackson's 99, two other candidates sharing an aggregate of 91,000 popular and 78 electoral votes. But the winner was determined by the House of Representatives, because no candidate had polled a majority. The House chose Adams over Jackson.

In 1876, Republican Rutherford B. Hayes was elected with 4.04 million popular votes to Democrat Samuel J. Tilden's 4.28 million. On election night the outcome was still in dispute with totals from Florida, Louisiana, and South Carolina as yet undecided. A special electoral commission was formed to apportion the unassigned nineteen electoral votes still at issue. In a political quid pro quo, the Southern Democrats agreed to back the Republican in exchange for the removal of federal troops from the South and an end to Reconstruction. Hayes became president with 185 electoral votes to Tilden's 184.

In 1888, Grover Cleveland lost with 5.54 million popular votes to Benjamin Harrison's 5.44 million. But Harrison received 233 electoral votes and Cleveland only 168.

This discordance between electoral and popular vote totals has repeatedly brought into question the electoral system, some factions of American politics arguing that it should be replaced by simple majority rule in the election of presidents.

CAMPAIGN PROMISES

Do you, as a voter, have any recourse when you discover that a candidate has misrepresented himself or herself to you in a campaign? Do you have any right of expectation that a campaigner will live up to his or her pledges once he or she assumes office? Can you force him or her to fulfill the declarations he or she made while trolling for your support? Can you take his or her mendacity as a personal deception? **Don't believe you can.**

In 1912, a voter in New York State became angered at a candidate who failed to fulfill his campaign obligations after he had taken office. The voter reasoned that he had given his vote in exchange for oral promises made by the campaigner, a quid pro quo, which thus constituted a verbal contract between the candidate and the voter. Disillusioned, he brought suit against the newly elected politician on grounds of breach of oral contract.

The judge disagreed. In a decision that still rankles today, the court ruled that a contract "cannot be based on an ante-election promise to voters generally by a candidate for public office, so as to give a voter a right to restrain the promiser from violating same." Which means simply that there is no legal recourse by which the electorate can pressure a candidate to live up to his or her campaign pledges, so politicians are free to say whatever they please in order to solicit votes without any obligation to fulfill their promises once in office. And candidates apparently know this, or at least act as if they do.

Where once our country had statesmen, now all we have are politicians.

For anyone who would like to read the full court opinion, the case can be found under the citation: *O'Reilly v. Mitchell*, 85 Misc. 176, 148 N.Y.S. 88 [Sup.Ct. 1914].

LOTTERIES

{ Government-run lotteries are a phenomenon of the twentieth century, the first being in New Hampshire in 1964.
Don't you believe it. }

National or regional lotteries have existed for centuries. Evidence of lotteries funding governmental programs dates from the Han Dynasty in China in the second century B.C.E.; one such lottery helped finance the Great Wall of China. Ancient Rome used a lottery to finance municipal upkeep and to distribute slaves. In the fifteenth century, the Dutch conducted lotteries to fund town fortifications and to help the poor. Queen Elizabeth I created a lottery to pay for public works in the sixteenth century; two hundred years later the British Museum was built with lottery income. In the nineteenth century, Italy helped support the state with the first national lottery.

So history reveals a long, if not laudable, record of several governments venturing into the gambling business.

In this country, before governmental activities could be adequately financed by taxation, lotteries were enacted for all kinds of civic projects and improvements. An early lottery was authorized by the Continental Congress to support the military. In the first half of the nineteenth century, well over a hundred lotteries by the states financed the creation and maintenance of public structures and other facilities. In 1985 the first multistate lottery was formed, running in three New England States.

Throughout this entire period the objections of antilottery forces were muted because the influx of money overshadowed the perceived immorality of government-sponsored public gambling. The situation has not changed noticeably at the present time, with a vast majority of states in the lottery business.

HYDROPHOBIA

The word *hydrophobia* elicits terrible images of victims gasping for breath and writhing on the ground. Translated from the Latin, the word *hydrophobia* means fear of water. But is that really an accurate description of what the disease entails?
Don't you believe it.

One of the most dreaded ailments of humanity throughout history has been rabies, or, as it is often called, hydrophobia. Until Louis Pasteur developed a method of preventing the disease by inoculation in the 1880s, there was little in the physician's armamentarium that could be used to relieve its painful symptoms and the inevitable paralysis and death that followed.

Rabies is an acute infectious disease that can attack all warm-blooded animals, not only humans. Once it was believed that the disease could be transmitted only by the bite of a rabid dog, but medical science has discovered that the pathogen can be carried in the saliva of several different species of animals.

The disease is caused by a virus that strikes the salivary glands and produces profound disturbance in the nervous system. The victim exhibits fever, excitability, aggressiveness, and, because of swelling in the throat and spasms in the muscles that control swallowing, is unable to drink urgently needed water.

The grimacing contortions the victim exhibits in fruitless attempts to take in the water he or she craves may look to the casual observer like a rejection, or a fear, of the water he or she is physically incapable of swallowing. And so, from the apparent demeanor of the sufferer, rabies has taken on the name of hydrophobia, or water fear, a distinctly inaccurate designation.

YET MORE QUICKIES

Ferdinand Magellan, credited with being the first to circum-navigate the globe, never made it. He was killed by Philippine natives in 1521. And only one of his five ships completed the first voyage around the world.

In spite of his bravado, Ernest Hemingway never fought in any war. In World War I he drove an ambulance for the American Red Cross. A week before his nineteenth birthday he was wounded by an artillery round, but as a noncombatant. During the Spanish Civil War and World War II he served as a reporter.

Shaving doesn't make the beard grow quicker or thicker. Cutting hairs that have already grown out has no affect on the follicles that produce them.

Pigs are thought of as dirty animals (they are not) because they have an affinity for mud pools; but so do some starlets and pampered women of wealth.

The same nominal amount is not always counted the same in different countries. In the United States, a billion is a thousand millions; in Great Britain a billion is a million millions.

Ellery Queen, the author of several mystery novels and stories, was not a real person. He was two people: cousins Frederic Dannay and Manfred B. Lee.

Alfred Nobel did not invent nitroglycerine. He is known for having invented dynamite.

When Coca-Cola was introduced in the late 1880s, its "medicinal" properties were enhanced by the inclusion of cocaine in the nonalcoholic "brain tonic." After the addictive nature of the drug was recognized, it was removed from the formula in the early 1900s.

An electric eel really is capable of giving a person a serious shock. Its organs are able to produce 450 to 600 volts.

JEFFERSON'S DECLARATION OF INDEPENDENCE

{
Thomas Jefferson's Declaration of Independence was an admirable example of original thinking, replete with new ideas and novel concepts.
Don't you believe it.
}

Jefferson's historic proclamation, which expounded the colonists' need for separation from Britain in favor of the creation of an independent nation, drew freely from a number of previous documents. Many of the ideas, particularly that relating to a theory of natural rights, were influenced by the writings of the seventeenth-century English philosophers Thomas Hobbes and John Locke, especially in Locke's *Second Treatise on Government*. In that tract Locke introduced the principle of the "social contract," an understanding by which government is granted by the people and under which the rights and duties of both the people and the government, and their respective limits, are defined and agreed upon. Much the same concepts are in Jefferson's introduction to the declaration.

Further, in May 1776, several weeks before the Continental Congress elected to declare the colonies' independence from Britain, Virginia had asserted its own independence in a document known as the Virginia declaration of Rights, prepared by George Mason.

Jefferson no doubt had read the Mason draft and drew on some of the ideas contained therein. A comparison of the opening text of the Virginia declaration and Jefferson's declaration reveals striking similarities between the two. Apparently, both men reflected the same zeitgeist.

None of this should disparage Jefferson's contribution. Even if the ideas he expounded were not totally novel, his document still stands equally as a political and literary accomplishment, both in exposition and clarity.

THE DEVIL'S BIBLE

{ The Bible is an infallible source of moral instruction. **Don't you believe it** . . . unless you have the proper edition. }

One of the most influential sections of this masterful work contains the Ten Commandments, which collectively form the basis of ethical conduct in Western society. But printers' errors can crop up even in such a revered volume, notably when human fallibility rears its unpredictable head. In the 1631 edition of the *King James Bible* (KJV), the edition now known as "The Devil's Bible" or "The Wicked Bible," Exodus 20:14 omitted a small word. The text was the seventh commandment, and the word was "not," changing the prescription to "Thou shalt commit adultery." The absence of only three letters can produce a critical ethical dilemma.

That, however, was not the only KJV with an egregious error. In a 1653 edition, now called the "Unrighteous Bible," a passage in 1 Corinthians 6:9 reads, "The unrighteous shall inherit the kingdom of God," the word "not" being omitted between "shall" and "inherit."

In a 1717 edition, known as the "Vinegar Bible," the word "vineyard" was replaced in Luke 20 to produce the title "The Parable of the Vinegar."

In a 1795 edition, called the "Murderer's Bible," Jesus is quoted as saying, "Let the children first be killed" (in Mark 7:27) instead of, "Let the children first be filled."

In the "Lion's Bible" of 1804, 1 Kings 8:19 reads, "Thy son shall come forth out of thy lions," instead of "thy loins."

But a 1702 printing contains an error that, given all the typos that have crept into other editions, speaks an unanticipated yet revealing truth: "Printers have persecuted me without cause," the word "printers" falsely replacing "princes."

PRESIDENT FILLMORE'S BATHTUB

{
In 1851, president Millard Fillmore installed the first bathtub in the White House.
Don't you believe it.
}

The story was made up by newspaperman H. L. Mencken, who had playfully created it as an anniversary retrospective for the *New York Evening Mail* on a quiet news day in 1917. According to Mencken's invented history, the first bathtub in America was installed in the home of a Cincinnati businessman in 1842, he having been impressed with one in England a dozen years earlier. As the story goes, the bathtub quickly grew in popularity and was soon appearing in wealthier homes. Medical authorities reviled it as a health hazard; in 1845, it was banned in Boston. But its respectability was established when Fillmore, on a trip to Cincinnati, tried the tub and became its "ardent advocate," ordering one for the White House when he became president.

Mencken's tongue-in-cheek hoax was accepted as fact by the reading public and by academic authorities alike. The details were reprinted in other newspapers, in scholarly publications and encyclopedias, and even in medical journals. Once the fire was set, it was impossible to extinguish. In 1926, Mencken wrote a disclaimer that appeared in several dozen newspapers across the country in which he exposed his prank and its repercussions. But his renunciation did little to stem the tale's growth.

In his 1958 book *Hoaxes*, Professor Curtis MacDougall prepared a chronology of over fifty publications from 1926, after Mencken's self-exposure up to the book's press time, that still alluded to the "facts" of his story.

Just for the record, running water and the first bath were both brought into the White House by Andrew Jackson.

WHO INVENTED BASEBALL?

{ It is a given that baseball was invented by Abner Doubleday in 1839 at Cooperstown, New York. **Don't you believe it.** }

Few historical facts are more ingrained in the American ortho-doxy, but, alas, Doubleday had nothing to do with the game.

American baseball has its nearest ancestry in an English game called rounders, a version of which, called town ball, was played in America around 1800. Both draw on an earlier English game called stoolball, in which one player throws a ball at a "stool" while another player, a batter, tries to prevent the ball from hitting it. "Stool" may have meant an actual milking stool or a tree stump, since the word also means a stump or the base of some plants. Several versions of stoolball existed, some including the batter running between two stools, somewhat like cricket.

The main difference between English rounders and American baseball is that in the English game the fielder could put out a runner by hitting him with a thrown ball that was originally a fielded grounder.

Printed rules for rounders have existed since 1828; references to stoolball date back to the eleventh century. A 1744 children's book published in England mentions a game called "base-ball," but in the absence of any explication we do not know how, or if, it related to the game that is played today.

How then was Doubleday credited with inventing the game? In 1907 a special Baseball Commission, established to verify its origins, concluded that Doubleday did indeed create the game. But the finding is suspect; many believe the commission was founded for the sole purpose of declaring the game an American invention.

The evidence for designating Doubleday as the inventor came exclusively from a letter the commission received from one Abner

Graves, who claimed he had been a schoolmate of Doubleday's and was present at Cooperstown when the game was devised. But it is now known that no member of the commission ever met with Graves nor had any follow-up communication with him, even at a distance.

It should be noted that Graves was five years old in 1839, the year he would have witnessed the game's creation, fifteen years younger than Doubleday, who was enrolled at West Point at the time and would not likely have been at Cooperstown. Further, Doubleday, who later enjoyed a distinguished military career, left an extensive collection of letters and diaries on his death in 1893, none of which included any claim to have created baseball, or indeed made any mention of it. His obituary in the *New York Times* makes no reference to the game, nor is he represented as an honoree in the Baseball Hall of Fame.

In fact, the Baseball Hall of Fame calls Alexander J. Cartwright "The Father of Modern Baseball," who, if he did not invent the game, at least gave it a structure that is recognizable today. His Hall of Fame biography credits Cartwright with playing a key role "in formalizing the first published rules of the game, including the concept of foul territory, the distance between the bases [and] three-out innings." Pitching at the time was underhand and a three-strikes-and-out rule applied to the striker [batter]. The rules were written in 1845 for the first organized baseball club, the New York Knickerbockers, of which Cartwright was a founding and influential member.

But some myths die hard. Although the legendary Doubleday/baseball connection has now been severed, there is little doubt that the same story will be told by future generations of baseball fans.

GONE FISHIN'

{
Here is a fish story that didn't make most news services.

This is one you can believe.
}

Fishing, we know, is a source of much of the world's food supply. But it is also a contemplative sport for millions of people around the globe. Among its virtues are its ability to provide relaxation, to allow one to enjoy the wonders of nature free from worldly cares and develop some great reminiscences about confrontation with the wild world. But sometimes a fisherman can be *too* engrossed in what he is doing.

In 1999, the Bloomberg News Source picked up an item from the *Deutsche Press-Agentur* about one such inventive, if careless, angler. Reporting on a bulletin from the Ukraine, the dispatch recounted the story of a man in Kiev who, fishing in the River Tereblya, reasoned that he could increase his catch by creatively employing the force of electricity. He connected cables to the main energy supply line for his home and extended them into the river, producing an electric charge that killed several fish, which then rose belly-up to the surface of the water ready to be netted.

He was delighted both to observe the large size of his catch waiting to be gathered and to recognize his own ingenuity in the innovative way he was able to harness the power of electricity for such a practical purpose. He congratulated himself on his ingenuity. But his elation was short lived when he took the next step—out of his boat and into the water to harvest his catch. In his enthusiasm, he had neglected to remove the live cables, and along with his piscine crop he fell victim to his own deadly inventiveness.

A fish story with a truly shocking ending that, unfortunately, he never got to tell anyone.

THE ROUND TABLE

The great table reputed to be the Round Table from King Arthur's court is on display in Hampshire, England, at what remains of Winchester Castle, which some believe is the location of what had been called Camelot. But is this really *the* Round Table? **Don't you believe it.**

The eighteen-foot-diameter table hanging in Winchester Castle's great hall has a prominent inscription in the center that reads, "This is the rownde table of kyng Arthur w(ith) xxiiii of his namyde knyattes." Around the outer rim, surrounding a depiction of Arthur, are recorded the names of twenty-four knights, presumptively those of Arthur's assembly.

Though written in an earlier form of English, the names translate to: Sir Galahad, Sir Lancelot du Lac, Sir Gawain, Sir Percivale, Sir Lionell, Sir Bors de Ganis, Sir Kay, Sir Tristram de Lyones, Sir Gareth, Sir Bedivere, Sir Bleoberis, La Cote Male Taile, Sir Lucan, Sir Palomedes, Sir Lamorak, Sir Safer, Sir Pelleas, Sir Ector de Maris, Sir Dagonet, Sir Degore, Sir Brunor le Noir, le Bel Desconneu, Sir Alymere, and Sir Mordred.

While the names are generally consistent with other lists of King Arthur's knights, the source of the table is unclear. According to Malory's *Le Morte d'Arthur*, the original Round Table was a wedding gift from Leodegrance, Guinevere's father. But authorities are certain this is not the same table. Dating tests have marked this table from the fourteenth century, hundreds of years after the time Arthur is believed to have lived.

Which raises another question to consider: Did King Arthur really exist?

Nonetheless, the Winchester Table, though not the Round Table of Arthurian legend, regularly attracts large crowds intrigued by tales of Camelot.

UNELECTED PRESIDENT

{

Gerald Ford is said to be the only president who was not elected to the executive branch of our government.
Don't you believe it.

}

Ford was appointed vice president by Richard Nixon to replace Spiro Agnew, who had resigned in disgrace. Ford's was the first such appointment under the Twenty-fifth Amendment. He succeeded to the presidency on August 9, 1974, after Nixon resigned following the Watergate scandal.

But Ford's ascendancy was not a unique occurrence.

On March 4, 1849, president-elect Zachary Taylor was scheduled to take the oath of office at 12:00 noon, when James Polk's term expired. But March 4 fell on a Sunday, and Taylor, who was a religious man, refused to dishonor the Sabbath by engaging in such a secular ritual. Ordinarily, the vice president, then George M. Dallas, would fill the position in the absence of the president, but his term expired the same time as Polk's. Thus, under the act of succession in force at that time, the next in line was president Pro Tem of the Senate, Senator David Rice Atchison of Missouri, who at noon automatically assumed the office of president of the United States.

Atchison, apparently, accepted his new position graciously. He met with a number of old friends and then retired for the day to sleep away the rest of his twenty-four-hour administration. The next day, March 5, at noon, Taylor took the oath and began his term, ending what was the shortest presidency in the history of the country.

Some historians argue that Atchison also had not taken the oath and therefore should not be considered a valid president, but he did legally hold the office under the amended rules of succession, even if he chose not to exercise it.

STARVE A FEVER, FEED A COLD

{ One of the most prevalent health nostrums offered by well-meaning friends and relatives is "Starve a fever, feed a cold." Or maybe "Starve a cold, feed a fever." Does either have any medical merit?
Don't you believe it. }

Whichever doesn't matter, because either way the bromide is pure myth. Physicians have long tried to stamp out this bit of dubious wisdom, but it seems ingrained in modern folklore.

So where did the saying originate? The part about starving has been traced back to a 1574 dictionary by a man named Withals, who wrote, "Fasting is a great remedie of feuer." The idea may be rooted in ancient medicine that believed food was fuel that helped maintain body temperature. Without fuel, the temperature would drop. With fuel, the body would warm to fight a cold.

The source of the other half of the phrase lies in well-deserved obscurity. There is a modicum of truth in the idea of starving a fever, in that people who are running an elevated temperature usually do not feel much like eating, while those with a cold (typically without fever) still do have an appetite.

In February 2007, the *New York Times* reported a Dutch research study that suggested eating increases the type of immune response that defends against viruses associated with colds, while fasting seemed to produce an immune response that may help the body guard against infections responsible for most fevers. But the study has gained little credence, because the sample was too small to provide definitive results and the research has not been replicated.

Authorities agree on only one proven treatment for both colds and fever: plenty of rest and nonalcoholic, noncaffeinated fluids.

CUSTER'S LAST STAND

> General George A. Custer and two hundred of his
> troopers were massacred at the Little Bighorn in 1876
> in what has become known as Custer's Last Stand.
> Common knowledge. But the assertion is tainted by
> two inaccuracies. So—
> **Don't you believe it.**

George Custer was not a general when he met his death
during the action at the Little Bighorn River. Custer was a
product of West Point, graduating at the bottom of his class, who
went on to repeatedly distinguish himself in several major battles
of the Civil War, including Bull Run, Antietam, Chancellorsville,
and Gettysburg. Known for his aggressive fearlessness on the
battlefield, he quickly rose through the ranks with brevet promo-
tions from lieutenant to captain to brigadier general of volunteers,
becoming at twenty-three one of the youngest generals in the
Union army. Just before cessation of hostilities, he was promoted
once again, this time to major general of volunteers.

When the war ended, Custer's battlefield commission expired
and he returned to the Regular Army with the permanent rank
of captain. Later, he was given command of the Seventh Cavalry
regiment and advanced in rank to lieutenant colonel, the grade he
held when he fought in the Indian Wars. In the military custom of
the times, he would frequently be called "General" in recognition
of his former brevet rank.

When Custer's force entered the northern plains in 1874,
he was still a lieutenant colonel and remained so when he was
defeated at the Little Bighorn by the Lakota Sioux and Cheyenne
under Chief Sitting Bull.

But the outcome cannot accurately be called a massacre;
rather it was a battlefield defeat of an armed military force in a
hostile action.

JULY FOURTH

{

The Continental Congress, meeting in Philadelphia, voted for independence on July 4, 1776, a day we celebrate as a national holiday.
Don't you believe it.

}

Contrary to what some history books tell us, the vote for independence was taken on July 2, not July 4.

The date of that fateful vote is recorded in a report that night in the *Pennsylvania Evening Post*. Further confirmation appears in a letter from John Adams to his wife Abigail in which he speculated, "The second day of July . . . will be celebrated by succeeding generations as the great anniversary festival." Celebration, yes; but not on that date. Why?

The explanation lies in the coexistence of two different proposals presented to the Continental Congress. One, offered in June by Richard Henry Lee of Virginia, was a resolution asserting independence. The other originated a few days later when a committee was appointed by Congress and charged with preparing a statement of rationale for the move to independence.

On July 2 Congress voted to adopt the Lee resolution. The other, a document written mostly by Thomas Jefferson, known as the Declaration of Independence, was accepted with some alteration by Congress on July 4, two days after passage of the Lee resolution. On July 2 Congress moved to break away from Great Britain; on July 4 Congress declared the reasons for what it had done on July 2.

Thus, the Fourth of July, in fact, celebrates the acceptance of the Declaration of Independence rather than the confirmation of the independence declaration. It does seem odd: rather than commemorating the momentous event that gave birth to our nation, we commemorate instead the document explaining the reason for that event.

"DEWEY DEFEATS TRUMAN"

{ Scientific polling is a good way to get an accurate assessment of people's prevailing preferences and attitudes.
Don't you believe it. }

No matter the controls built into the process, the most scientific of polls can be wrong. Sometimes very wrong.

The experts were all wrong about the 1948 presidential election, in which incumbent Harry S Truman ran against Republican Thomas E. Dewey. All poll results indicated Dewey was a shoo-in. About eight weeks before election day, pollster Elmo Roper announced there would no more polling on this election. He is quoted as saying, "My whole inclination is to predict the election of Thomas E. Dewey by a heavy margin and devote my time and efforts to other things."

At about the same time, the widely read *Life* magazine had Dewey appearing on the cover with a caption that read, "The next President of the United States." And the venerable *New York Times* declared, "Thomas E. Dewey's election as president is a foregone conclusion."

Everyone believed that Truman had no chance; everyone, that is, except Truman. He began a "whistle-stop campaign," traveling the country by rail, stopping at town after town, shaking hands, and talking with the voters. But his poll numbers trailed Dewey's. While Truman was still on his tour, *Newsweek* polled fifty leading political writers to sample their predictions on which candidate would win. In its October 11 issue, *Newsweek* released the results: all fifty expected the winner would be Dewey.

But they were all wrong. Truman won and was photographed holding a copy of the election day *Chicago Daily Tribune* with the headline, "Dewey Defeats Truman."

A leading columnist wrote, "The fatal flaw was the reliance on the public opinion polls."

BAKER'S DOZEN

{
The baker's dozen developed as a competitive mar-
keting contrivance.
Don't you believe it.
}

The baker's dozen is one more than the usual dozen. As a unit, it dates back several centuries. It is frequently assumed that this measure originated as a ploy by medieval bakers to maintain the loyalty of their customers by adding a lagniappe loaf of bread with each twelve loaves purchased.

But the truth is more complicated than that. The additional loaf had important ramifications under the laws and penalties of the time.

Either inadvertently or intentionally, bakers in medieval England not infrequently sold loaves under the usual weight. A small amount saved per loaf could add to a considerable amount saved over several loaves. But bread was a staple of the diet, and the government recognized the need to establish standards for its weight and pricing. In 1266, during the reign of Henry III, an English law—the Assize of Bread—set the required standards and prescribed severe penalties for short-weighting loaves. Heavy fines and physical punishment were not uncommon. The baker could be pilloried for a first offense, and run out of town if he persisted in overcharging.

But given the poor education of most bakers and the rudimentary bakery technology of the time, it was difficult even for honest practitioners to bake breads of uniform weight. So bakers—ever mindful of the punishment awaiting them for selling undersize loaves—added a thirteenth loaf to every order of twelve. It was safer to be overweight than under. Thus the term "baker's dozen" meaning thirteen.

The term has persisted and now applies to any merchandise sold in quantities of thirteen.

THREE-DIMENSIONAL BASEBALL

{ Baseball is a game in which only two teams can play in opposition, alternately taking turns batting and fielding; two teams, according to the rules of the game, with no variations possible.
Don't you believe it. }

Actually, there was a special occasion during which the basic rules were disregarded.

On June 26, 1944, during World War II, a highly unusual exhibition game was played at the Polo Grounds, the bygone stadium of the old New York Giants on 157th Street in Manhattan. The extraordinary contest had the Giants playing against the Yankees playing against the Dodgers playing against the Giants. No, not a misprint—there really was a unique three-way game, an event sponsored by the War Bond Sports Committee to raise money for the war effort. The nine-inning game was structured so that each team played consecutive innings against the other two teams and then sat out an inning.

In addition to the game, the day was further enlivened by a series of field event competitions: fungo batting, throwing for accuracy, and a sprint contest.

More than fifty thousand attendees contributed a total of $5.5 million to see the once-in-a-lifetime game. The Bond Clothing Company paid $1 million for an autographed program. But the bulk of the contribution came from the City of New York, under Mayor Fiorello La Guardia, which supported the event by purchasing $50 million worth of war bonds.

When the smoke had cleared and the teams had tallied up their runs, the final scores were logged in as Dodgers 5, Yankees 1, Giants 0. An unusual tripartite datum for the record books, one not to be repeated. The day was a memorable experience for the fans who witnessed this truly historic baseball event.

GEORGE WASHINGTON AND THE CHERRY TREE

{

"I cannot tell a lie. I did it." So, we are told, said Master George Washington when his father asked if it was he who had chopped down the cherry tree. Surely a paragon of truthfulness and responsibility, an admirable display of character. the personification of honesty—a model for every young American to follow. But did it ever really happen?

Don't you believe it.

}

The tale of Washington and the cherry tree first appeared in the 1806 sixth edition of *The Life of George Washington, with Curious Anecdotes Laudable to Himself and Exemplary to His Countrymen*, by Mason Locke Weems. It is worth noting that it was not included in the five earlier editions. According to Weems, the young Washington was charged not with cutting down the cherry tree, but with killing it.

Historians have been unable to substantiate the event and, in the absence of any evidence that it really happened, they generally discount its historical verity, although they laud its inspirational value. It should be noted that Weems' book was written at a time when it was common for biographers to portray the early Americans with saintly virtues and to inflate their godliness, describing them with flattering attributes. And Weems is known for having embellished other of his historical narratives.

Nonetheless, the story quickly captured the national imagination as a morality tale and persists to this day, even in the absence of any confirmation.

However, no one has ever been able to definitively discount the possibility that it actually occurred. So truth lies in the eyes of the beholder. Is it history or myth? We will probably never know. Anyway, it makes for a good story.

THE SHORTEST WAR

{ The 1967 Six-Day War between Israel and its surrounding Arab nations was a decisive, but brief, conflict—probably the shortest war on record. **Don't you believe it.** }

Seventy years earlier, the United Kingdom and Zanzibar fought a war of considerably shorter duration.

On August 25, 1896, Sultan Hamad bin Thuwaini of Zanzibar died. For centuries the rulers of Zanzibar had been chosen by the important clans, and in this instance they favored as his successor Hamad's nephew, Khalid bin Barghash. However, Barghash was too independent-minded for the British, and in his place the British consul named as the new leader another nephew, Hamoud bin Muhammed, who they knew was much more likely to bend to British control. But Barghash moved quickly to occupy the royal palace, claiming the throne as grandson of Sayyid Said, the founder of the country.

When the British unilaterally rejected their choice, the Zanzibari leaders saw it as unacceptable interference in their traditional rights.

The British authorities demanded Khalid's resignation. He refused, and the British gave him an ultimatum coming due on August 27 at 9:00 AM. If Khalid did not evacuate within the next forty hours, the British fleet would blast him out.

About an hour before the deadline was reached, Khalid tried to negotiate a peaceful end to the standoff by contacting the local American representative, who refused to intercede. A few minutes after the deadline, British warships in the harbor began shelling the palace, all but destroying it in short order. Khalid fled to the German consulate, where he was granted asylum.

The entire confrontation had lasted thirty-eight minutes, the shortest war in recorded history.

THE JEWISH CARDINAL

{
A Jewish Cardinal of the Catholic Church? Is it
an anomaly? A Jewish Archbishop of Paris? Is it
possible?
You can believe it.
}

As unlikely as it sounds, both existed, and both were the
same person. Aaron Lustiger was born of Polish Jewish parents
in Paris in September 1926. In 1939, at the outbreak of World
War II, his family relocated to Orleans, where he was attracted to
Catholicism and opted to convert. His family first objected, then
finally accepted his decision, seeing his conversion as a defense
against growing anti-Semitic persecution. At fourteen he was
baptized Aaron Jean-Marie Lustiger by the bishop of Orleans.

He went on from there—ordained a priest in 1954, a bishop
in 1979, appointed Archbishop of Paris in January 1981, and
Cardinal in February 1983—the only Cardinal to speak fluent
Yiddish. As a close associate of Pope John Paul II, Lustiger was
frequently mentioned as a possible successor. Throughout, he
affirmed his Jewish heritage.

Lustiger retired in March 2005; he died in August 2007. His
epitaph, which he wrote himself, says: "I was born Jewish. . . .
Having become Christian by faith and by Baptism, I have remained
Jewish as did the Apostles." On his death, the World Jewish
Congress paid homage to him.

His father and sister survived the war, but his mother died at
the Auschwitz concentration camp in 1943.

Lustiger was one of only two Catholic prelates in modern
times—the other was Jean-Baptiste Gourion, bishop of
Jerusalem—who were born Jewish and still considered themselves
Jewish. Scores of Jews have converted to Catholicism, some acting
out of deep belief, some to escape Nazi brutality. But none other
achieved such rank in the Church hierarchy.

PROGNOSTICATION

{ Could it be that sometimes we, or maybe others more
gifted, are really able to predict the future?
Don't you believe it. }

We all have that feeling, occasionally. It is correct sometimes, erroneous far more often. Otherwise, gamblers and stock investors would be considerably richer than they are. And international relations would be much improved if negotiators could accurately foresee the other party's intentions and divine the vagaries of the opposition diplomacy.

Nostradamus is frequently cited as a paragon of prognostication. But anyone who has read the work of Nostradamus knows that his predictions were couched in such vague terms and were so open to vastly differing interpretation that they could be applied virtually anywhere at any time to any occurrence.

And what about the professional soothsayers? Has anyone tracked their success rate? How about fortune tellers? Palm readers? Crystal ball enthusiasts? Astrologers? We note, for example, that TV's Psychic Network went bankrupt, apparently without the parties having any foreknowledge that it was about to happen.

But one little-known case is worth reporting in defense of prophecy. Early one January a Mr. Willis Jaffe of Hollis, Long Island, predicted that the world would come to an end on September 16. For several months he tried to publicize his message but no one, not even the media, gave it any credence. By that August, rebuffed innumerable times, he began to doubt his own ability to foresee future events. Then, on a fateful day, September 16, Mr. Jaffe walked out of his home, crossed the street, and was struck by a truck and killed instantly.

We offer this as one of the rare cases of someone accurately seeing into the future.

DAVY CROCKETT

{ Davy Crockett, "king of the wild frontier," died heroically in battle defending the Alamo against the onslaught of superior Mexican forces under General Antonio López de Santa Ana.
Don't you believe it. }

That he died at the Alamo is confirmed; how he did so is open to question.

Crockett was one of two hundred men defending the mission at San Antonio against the Mexican Army of several thousand. But records indicate that Crockett may not have died the glorious death that is portrayed in several films and historical novels.

A diary kept by Mexican Lieutenant Colonel José Enrique de la Peña, a combatant in the Alamo confrontation, tells a different story. According to de la Peña's eyewitness account, Crockett and six others survived the battle and were captured by the Mexican forces. But Santa Ana had ordered that no prisoners be taken, and, angered that his command had not been faithfully followed, he directed that all six be executed. The de la Peña diary recounts how the six were bayoneted and then shot.

Inasmuch as the diary contradicts the lofty tale of Crockett nobly fighting to the death, it has aroused serious controversy and its authenticity has been disputed. But analysis of the paper and ink of the diary have confirmed they were both of the period and not likely later counterfeits. Indeed, in his introduction to the recent edition of the diary, professor James E. Crisp, of the North Carolina State University history department, and a native of Texas, has proclaimed it genuine.

That de la Peña was not attempting to demean Crockett's distinction as a courageous warrior is evidenced by his disavowal of the execution and his admiration of Crockett's "stoic" acceptance of his ultimate fate.

MASON-DIXON LINE

{ The Mason-Dixon line was established to define a border between the slave colonies of the South and the nonslave colonies of the North.
Don't you believe it. }

When astronomer Charles Mason and surveyor Jeremiah Dixon performed their survey in the mid-1760s, the sole purpose was to settle a contested property border. They were asked to lay stone markers at one-mile intervals to define the 233-mile boundary between the colonies of Pennsylvania and Maryland. There was as yet no United States, only separate colonies, and the line had nothing to do with slavery. In fact, at the time both Pennsylvania and Maryland retained slaves.

In 1632, King Charles I had given the colony of Maryland to George Calvert, the first Lord Baltimore. Fifty years later, in 1682, King Charles II gave William Penn the territory to the north, which later became Pennsylvania. But the two land grants were imprecise, containing conflicting property descriptions, and the confusion resulted in hotly contested land disputes between the two colonies; these disputes often erupted into violent confrontations. The survey was intended to settle the boundary and thus eliminate the source of conflict.

A half century later, the demarcation line assumed prominence with the Missouri Compromise of 1820, which fixed a boundary between the free states of the north and the slave states of the south. The boundary became known as the Mason-Dixon line, because it encompassed the border the two surveyors had established and extended the line westward to the Ohio River and then beyond. The name quickly attained a symbolic importance in the nation's struggle over the issue of slavery, an eponymous designation still bearing emotional overtones even to this day.

NAPOLEON IN RUSSIA

{
Napoleon's *Grand Armèe* was defeated in Russia by the brutal winter of 1812.
Don't you believe it.
}

Napoleon's troops crossed the Niemen River into Russian-controlled East Poland on June 24, encountering drenching thunderstorms and stifling heat. The roads, mostly dirt paths, soon became virtual swamps, preventing his supply carts from delivering needed provisions. But Napoleon expected the tsar to surrender after the first confrontation and he had not prepared for an extended campaign.

By the time the march on Moscow began, the *Grand Armèe* had shrunk to one-third of its original complement, having lost 35,000 troops in the battle of Borodino in mid-August and hundreds of thousands more to disease, starvation, and desertions. Napoleon's supply problems were exacerbated by Russian troops scorching the earth as they fell back before his advance, leaving little to be foraged.

When Napoleon entered Moscow on September 14, he found a city bereft of people and supplies. There was no Russian force to capitulate and no food to eat; rather, he was greeted with fires in much of the city, depriving his soldiers also of shelter.

With Russian forays choking his meager supply lines, winter threatening, and no sign of obvious victory, in mid-October Napoleon finally decided to abandon the city and retrace his steps. The retreat began.

But October was unusually warm. Winter did not appear until November 6, by which time Napoleon's troops were in total disarray, the remaining horses having been killed for food by starving troops. Although weakened soldiers succumbed to the intense cold that followed, the wintry conditions was not the cause of their defeat but only aggravated their already miserable situation.

GENERAL GRANT DECLINES

{
General Ulysses S. Grant could have been killed with President Lincoln in the box at Ford's Theatre.
You can believe it.
}

It is a speculative scenario, but one truly possible. We don't know that Grant would have been killed, let alone shot, but the possibility arose when Lincoln invited Grant and his wife, Julia, to join him and Mrs. Lincoln in the presidential box to attend a performance of *Our American Cousin*.

General Grant had met with Robert E. Lee at Appomattox on April 9, 1865, to effect the surrender of Confederate forces, virtually ending the Civil War. Following the formalities of surrender, Grant proceeded to Washington to attend to some administrative military chores. Lincoln asked Grant if he would like to join the president and his wife at the theater on the 14th, but Grant instead chose to visit with his children in New York. He expressed his regrets, explaining his desire to spend some time with his family. Apparently, Lincoln appreciated Grant's dilemma and accepted his decision.

On April 14, President and Mrs. Lincoln attended Ford's Theatre to watch the play. With Lincoln in the presidential box, Booth made his way to the upper level, entered the box from the rear, and fired his derringer point-blank into the back of Lincoln's head, fatally wounding him.

We do not know what difference Grant's presence might have made. Would he have been a second victim? Could he have been able to stop the shooting? Might he have been able to save Lincoln's life, given his experience with wounded soldiers on the battlefield? Could he have at least deflected the shot, hereby limiting Lincoln's damage to a comparatively minor wound?

We will never know. But we do know that Grant chose not to attend.

CAPTAIN KIDD

{ Captain Kidd was a brutal pirate with loyalty to none
other than his own greed.
Don't you believe it. }

Many historians reject this characterization. They consider
Kidd a privateer, not a pirate—a significant distinction. Unlike
pirates, privateers were commissioned to attack ships of opposing
nations, usually backed by wealthy investors and frequently with
the protection of their sovereign. Profits were shared with their
backers and usually with the crown under whose authority they
sailed.

William Kidd was a successful merchant who was given a
commission both to hunt pirates and to capture French ships. He
left England in 1695 on the *Adventure Galley*, his voyage financed
by a group of Whig peers, including Sir George Bellomont
(the governor of New York and Massachusetts) and likely King
William—all for a share of the profits.

Kidd found few pirate ships, and when he refused to capture
British vessels, his crew grew mutinous. In confronting one muti-
neer, William Moore, Kidd hit him with a bucket and killed
him. Soon after, pressured by his crew, he managed to capture
a large ship, the *Quedah Merchant*, which, it turned out, carried
French papers. On returning, he entrusted the French passes to
Bellomont.

But Kidd fell victim to political warfare between the Tories
and the Whigs, several of whom had financed him, and when
he was arrested for piracy and for killing Moore, his backers
abandoned him to save their own reputations. The French passes
somehow disappeared, and Kidd could produce no evidence
against his charge of piracy.

In a rigged trial, he was found guilty on May 9, 1701,
protesting to the end that he was a privateer, not a pirate. He was
hanged on May 23 of that year.

RECYCLE NUMBERS

{
Those single digits shown in triangles on plastic containers tell the number of times the material has already been recycled.
Don't you believe it.
}

The numbers have nothing to do with previous recycling. Rather, they indicate the type of substance of which the item is composed, this seven-code schema developed by the Society of Plastics Engineers to identify specific materials. Inasmuch as each type of resin has its own distinctive properties, the number system provides a way to sort items into generally homogeneous groups for recycling:

1—polyethylene terephthalate (PETE): found in bottles for soda, water, and cooking oil, oven-ready meal trays, and peanut butter jars

2—high-density polyethylene (HDPE): detergent and shampoo bottles, milk jugs, and motor oil containers

3—polyvinyl chloride (V): clear food packaging, plastic pipes, and outdoor furniture

4—low density polyethylene (LDPE): frozen food bags, squeezable bottles, and dry-cleaning bags

5—polypropylene (PP): bottle caps, prescription bottles, plastic cups, and drinking straws

6—polystyrene (PS): disposable eating utensils; as Styrofoam it is used for coffee cups, meat trays, egg cartons, and anti-impact packaging forms

7—all others (OTHER) [plastic polymers & mixed resins]: some ketchup bottles, some food container lids, and Tupperware

A few localities do accept all types. However, most states or communities have their own recycling requirements for the different materials. The most common for recapture are types 1 and 2. Many supermarkets accept bags of types 3 or 4. Numbers 5 and 6 are usually consigned to the trash, as is type 7, which cannot be recycled and ordinarily ends up as landfill.

PENNSYLVANIA DUTCH

{
The Pennsylvania Dutch, who inhabit a good part of
the southeastern part of that state, are descendants of
early colonists from Holland.
Don't you believe it.
}

The so-called Pennsylvania Dutch are *not* Dutch at all, but
rather trace their ancestry to German settlers who arrived in the area
in the eighteenth century. Known also as Pennsylvania Germans,
the earliest arrivals—who located first in Germantown, later in
and around Lancaster—were largely Amish and Mennonites,
emigrants from the German Palatinate and the German-speaking
part of Switzerland, with a small share of German-speaking
French Huguenot refugees.

Then why the designation "Dutch"? Several theories exist.
Some experts believe the appellation is a corruption of "Deutsch,"
the German word for "German." Others trace the name to early
English usage, which referred to all people of Germanic heritage
as Dutch or Dutchmen, regardless of where on the Continent
they originated or resided. Still others believe the name was meant
as a convenience to distinguish Pennsylvania Germans from the
New York Dutch, the language of the two sounding similar to the
untrained ear.

The local acceptance of the designation was aided by the
occurrence of two world wars in which America fought against
Germany. Having established firm roots in this country, Pennsylvania Germans found it practical to obfuscate their German
ancestry to avoid any public backlash against an enemy nationality. And so the name has persisted over generations and today
describes a peaceful agrarian people who cling to the ways of the
old country. With time, however, their homogeneity is dimin-
ishing as the younger generation increasingly experiences the
wider world, intermarries with it, and moves away from the old
identity.

ONCE AGAIN, MORE QUICKIES

Probably the best known of India's leaders was Mahatma Gandhi. But Mahatma was not his name. His given name was Mohandas. Mahatma is a title of respect for a person revered for his wisdom and righteousness.

Cobras do not sway to the music of a snake charmer's flute, because the snakes have no ears and can't hear music. Rather, they are mimicking the movements of the undulating performer.

It is widely believed that Hitler's Germany suffered humiliation at the 1936 Olympics when a few black athletes captured several medals, piercing the myth of Teutonic superiority. However, records prove that Germany won more medals than any other nation, hardly a humiliating outcome.

There's no lead in a lead pencil. The writing material is a mixture of graphite and clay. The more graphite in the mixture, the softer the pencil is.

Wilt Chamberlain's incredible feat of scoring one hundred points in a single basketball game would seem to be an insurmountable record—except for college basketball's Clarence (Bevo) Francis of Rio Grande (Ohio) University, who put up 113 points against Hillsdale College on February 2, 1954.

Given the time required to count out a KO'd fighter, it would seem that a boxing match can't run less than ten seconds. Not true. The shortest fight on record took place at the Leisure Centre in Ebbw Vale, New Zealand, on November 3, 2000, when Russell Rees knocked out Des Snowden with his first punch in four seconds of the first round.

Florida's Everglades is thought of as an extensive swamp. But in reality the Everglades is a river—slow-moving, but a river nonetheless. Popularly called a river of grass, the phrase was popularized by Marjory Stoneman Douglas in her marvelous book, *The Everglades: River of Grass*.

THE DARK AGES

{
The intellectual rebirth of the Renaissance, following the sterility of the Dark Ages, was stimulated by the rediscovered remains of Latin learning in monastic safekeeping.
Don't you believe it.
}

Measured roughly from the fall of the Western Roman Empire in 476, the Dark Ages were characterized by superstition and ignorance. With the collapse of Rome came the cessation of cultural advancement.

Learning in the Western world was stifled by the ascendancy of the Church and its inhospitality to any ideas that did not conform to Church teaching. Independent thought was suppressed. Scientific findings were repudiated. The world was flat, the Earth was the center of the universe, Heaven was above the earth, and Hell was below it. Anyone voicing ideas that did not adhere to the teachings of Rome was in danger of retribution for heresy, and heretics were severely punished.

It was a world of faith rather than a world of reason; although, excluding the monastics, piety was not conspicuous.

After the sacking of the library at Alexandria in 642, hundreds of years of accumulated knowledge was either lost or dispersed. But the libraries at Baghdad and at Constantinople rescued much of Greek lore, and, in the centuries that followed, the Muslim world was rich in ideas in astronomy, mathematics, medicine, physics, and chemistry. The Arabs developed and expanded concepts they had learned from the Byzantine Greeks and, according to professor George Sarton, "rose to as high an intellectual level as any people has ever reached."

When the Crusaders returned from the east, they brought back intimations of the knowledge preserved in the Muslim world, sparking the Renaissance in Western Europe.

THE EXCEPTION PROVES THE RULE

{ "The exception proves the rule": one of the most quoted, and most misinterpreted, proverbs in the English language. Is the adage self-contradictory? **Don't you believe it.** }

On the surface, the phrase makes no sense. An exception cannot be used to prove a rule; the existence of an exception would seem rather to nullify a rule. The misunderstanding lies in the meaning of the word "prove," which, as used in mathematical inquiry and also as confirmed by the *Oxford English Dictionary*, originally meant to test the accuracy or characteristics of something. In this context, the phrase makes good sense: An exception definitely does test a rule.

The Latin root of the English word furnishes a clue to the confusion in interpreting the proverb. The Latin verb *probo* translates to English as test or approve and provides the basis for such English words as probe, probative, or probable. When one probes, one performs an exploratory investigation. In law, probate means to examine a will with the intention of approving it as genuine and valid. Probation defines a period during which a person is tried and tested to determine his or her fitness for a job, or school, or return to civil society. Thus, the meaning of the phrase takes on a new definition.

However, on reflection, a more subtle implication of the phrase presents itself. To accept the existence of an exception, it is necessary also to accept the existence of a rule to which the exception applies. One is the corollary of the other. Without a rule, no exception is possible.

All of which points out that the simplest proverbs should not be taken at face value. On reflection, one can frequently discern hidden implications that add significantly to their apparent meaning.

EISENHOWER'S MISGIVINGS

{
On the eve of the invasion of Europe in June 1944, General Eisenhower had misgivings about the outcome of the impending landings.
Don't you believe it.
}

Throughout the preparations for invasion, Ike felt assured of victory. His staff had planned for all contingencies down to the minutest detail and he was confident that the "Longest Day" would end successfully for his invading force. The rainy days that had preceded June 6 were about to end and clear weather was anticipated. Thousands of ships and planes were geared up and ready to go. Some three million men were in position, anxious to get into action. All was in readiness, awaiting only Eisenhower's signal to "go."

But as an experienced commander, he knew that even with the most meticulous planning the unexpected could possibly turn the invasion into a disaster. And he had to be prepared with a statement for such an unlikely eventuality.

The day before the landing on the continent, he scribbled a note that would be made public should the invasion fail. His prepared announcement was to be kept securely hidden unless it was needed.

Roger Bruns of the National Archives has uncovered Ike's handwritten note, which reads as follows:

"Our landings in the Cherbourg-Havre area have failed to gain a satisfactory foothold and I have withdrawn the troops. My decision to attack at this time and place was based upon the best information available. The troops, the air, and the Navy did all that Bravery and devotion to duty could do. If any blame or fault attaches to the attempt it is mine alone."

As we know, the landings were successful, and Ike's note became a mere sidelight to history.

"THERE'S A SUCKER BORN EVERY MINUTE"

{ Showman P. T. Barnum is best remembered for the observation, "There's a sucker born every minute." **Don't you believe it.** }

Because Barnum didn't really say it. It all happened as a side-light to the Cardiff Giant hoax. A man named George Hull, of Binghamton, New York, had a slab of gypsum carved in the shape of a huge human being, had the carved figure treated to resemble on ossified corpse, and buried it on a farm near Cardiff, New York. About a year later, in October 1969, the archeological artifact was "discovered" when the owner of the farm engaged some friends to help dig a well.

Newspapers everywhere picked up the story of the "Cardiff Giant," and soon thousands of the curious were paying fifty cents apiece to view the oddity. Hull then sold part ownership to a man named Hannum, who moved the giant to Syracuse and doubled the admission price to a dollar.

Barnum made an offer to buy the giant but was turned down. Not to be outdone, he had a duplicate giant carved, which he exhibited, claiming Hannum had sold the original to him and had replaced it with a fake on display. Newspapers picked up Barnum's version and the crowds started coming to see his giant. It was then that Hannum—not Barnum—was quoted as saying, "There's a sucker born every minute," assuming his giant was real and the thousands paying good money to see Barnum's fake were being ripped off.

Hannum sued Barnum for calling his giant a fake. In court the hoax was revealed and the judge ruled for Barnum, finding that the original Cardiff Giant *was* a fake and Barnum was thus not guilty of anything.

Hannum and Hull have long since been forgotten, but the "sucker" quote has stuck to Barnum instead.

SECTION TWO:
SAYS WHO?

MIMICKING BARNUM, DOZENS OF OTHER WELL-KNOWN QUOTATIONS WERE NOT SAID BY THE WELL-KNOWN PEOPLE TO WHOM THEY ARE ATTRIBUTED. ONCE A SAYING IS LINKED TO A CELEBRATED FIGURE, IT IS NIGH IMPOSSIBLE TO UNDO THE LINK, NO MATTER HOW OFTEN THE TRUTH IS REPEATED. CELEBRITY TRUMPS TRUTH WHEN IDENTIFYING THE SOURCE OF A GOOD APHORISM. READ ON.

A classic example of misattribution is the memorable phrase, "Let them eat cake," supposedly uttered by Marie Antoinette when told her subjects had no bread. But this most quotable quote first appeared, attributed merely to "a great princess," in Rousseau's *Confessions*, written several years before Marie had even arrived in France.

—∽∿∾—

"I disapprove of what you say, but I will defend to the death your right to say it." Voltaire is reputed to have written this in support of French philosopher Helvétius, who was vilified by the French Parliament for his book *On the Mind*. But Voltaire never wrote it. The line is actually from S. G. Tallentyre's *The Friends of Voltaire*, paraphrasing what the author thought Voltaire was thinking.

—∽∿∾—

"Lafayette, we are here." The words reportedly said by General John Pershing when the American Expeditionary Force landed in France during World War I. But Pershing later denied having said it and attributed the phrase to Lieutenant Colonel Charles E. Stanton, who Pershing asked to stand in for him at Lafayette's tomb on July 4, 1917.

—∽∿∾—

"A journey of a thousand miles begins with a single step," was not said by Confucius but by Lao-tzu, the founder of Taoism.

—∽∿∾—

Yes, John F. Kennedy, in his 1961 inaugural address, did speak the oft-quoted line, "Ask not what your country can do for you; ask what you can do for your country." But he was only paraphrasing president Warren Harding, who, some forty years earlier, had said, "Think more of what you can do for your government than of what your government can do for you."

⁓

Horace Greeley did not originate the admonition, "Go west, young man, go west." It first appeared in an article by John L. Soule in the *Terre Haute Express*, but Greeley, though he tried several times, was unable to disown it.

⁓

"Only the dead have seen the end of war." Inaccurately attributed to Plato in a speech by General Douglas MacArthur, this line is actually from George Santayana's 1924 *Soliloquies in England*.

⁓

Shakespeare is mistakenly cited as the author of more quotations than any other writer. A few examples: "Oh, what a tangled web we weave, When first we practice to deceive." (In truth, this is from Sir Walter Scott's *Marmion*); "War is the trade of kings." (From Dryden's *King Arthur II*, ii); "Music hath charms to soothe the savage breast." (Actually from William Congreve's *The Mourning Bride*); "Hell hath no fury like a woman scorned." (Also from the Congreve tragedy); "For want of a nail, the shoe is lost, for want of a shoe the horse is lost, for want of a horse the rider is lost." (This statement was really made by George Herbert, in *Jacula Prudentum*); "For you suffer fools gladly, seeing yourself as wise." (From the Bible, II Corinthians.) Dozens of others could be cited, but the point is made.

—∞—

"The only traditions of the Royal Navy are rum, sodomy, and the lash," are words attributed to Winston Churchill, who didn't say them but, according to his aide, Anthony Montague-Brown, said he wished he had. The sentiment, in slightly different terms, has been traced to a 1950 entry in the diary of English diplomatic theorist, Harold Nicolson.

—∞—

Nazi Hermann Goering is supposed to have said, "Whenever I hear the word 'culture,' I reach for my revolver." But if it sounds like something Goering would have uttered, it was actually said by a character in a 1933 play, *Schlageter*, by German playwright Hanns Johst.

—∞—

In his run for the presidency in 1928, Republican Herbert Hoover did not promise "a chicken in every pot and a car in every garage." The phrase comes from an ad placed by the Republican National Committee. What Hoover did say was, "The slogan of progress is changing from the full dinner pail to the full garage."

—∞—

Nowhere in Shakespeare's play does Macbeth say, "Lead on, Macduff." His actual words, in act V scene VIII, are, "Lay on, Macduff, and damn'd be him that first cries, '*Hold, enough!*'"

—⚏—

Mark Twain may have said, "Wagner's music is better than it sounds," but if he did, he was not the first to do so. He was quoting his contemporary, American humorist Bill Nye.

—⚏—

W. C. Fields' grave marker does not say, "I would rather be living in Philadelphia." Although he may have proposed this line as his epitaph, his tomb at Forest Lawn Cemetery in Glendale, California, simply reads, "W. C. Fields 1880–1946."

—⚏—

More W. C. Fields: "Anyone who hates dogs and children can't be all bad." Actually, the line was, "Any man who hates babies and dogs can't be all bad." And it wasn't said by Fields, but about him, by writer Leo Rosten, who used the line to introduce the comedian at a banquet.

—⚏—

Ralph Waldo Emerson is credited with the line, "Build a better mousetrap and the world will make a beaten path to your door." Emerson did write something very similar in his journal in

1855 but he didn't mention mousetraps. They were added by Sarah S. B. Yule and Mary S. Keene in their 1889 book *Borrowings*: "If a man can write a better book, preach a better sermon, or make a better mouse-trap than his neighbor, though he builds his house in the woods the world will make a beaten path to his door." Yule once said that Emerson had repeated it in one of his lectures.

—〜〜—

Napoleon may actually have said that the English were "a nation of shopkeepers." But if he did, he was quoting Adam Smith, who first used it in his *Wealth of Nations*.

—〜〜—

The organizing cry of the 1960s student rebellion, "Don't trust anyone over thirty," was not proffered by political activist Abbie Hoffman or Berkeley drop-out Jerry Rubin, but by their student collaborator Jack Weinberg in an interview with a *San Francisco Chronicle* reporter.

—〜〜—

The U.S. Constitution doesn't guarantee life, liberty, and the pursuit of happiness to American citizens. It's the Declaration of Independence, not the Constitution, that asserts that "all men are created equal, that they are endowed with certain inalienable rights, including life, liberty, and the pursuit of happiness, and that governments are instituted to secure those rights . . ."

—〜〜—

Several sayings that do not appear therein are nonetheless attributed to the Bible. Just a few: "Cleanliness is next to Godliness" (This is really from John Wesley's Sermon XCIII, *On Dress*.); "Gods help him who helps himself" (This phrase is attributed by different authorities to either Aesop or Euripides. In any case, it is early Greek. In later citations, "Gods" became singular as Western society turned monotheistic.); "Fools rush in where angels fear to tread" (From *An Essay on Criticism* by the British poet Alexander Pope.); "Spare the rod and spoil the child" (Actually an old English proverb, borrowed from Latin, and traced back to about 1000 C.E. But a somewhat similar sentiment does appear in the Bible, Proverbs 13:24, "He that spareth his rod hateth his son: but he that loveth him chasteneth him betimes.").

—∽—

Football coach Vince Lombardi is credited with the observation, "Winning isn't everything; it's the only thing." But it was actually said by Red Sanders, the coach of Vanderbilt and then UCLA football, quoted in *Sports Illustrated* in 1955.

—∽—

Microsoft's Bill Gates, often described as an admitted nerd, is credited with having said, "Be nice to nerds. Chances are you'll end up working for one." But although apparently in character, the quote did not come from Gates; it was actually said by Charles J. Sykes, a radio and television talk-show host and critic of American education.

—∽—

Mark Twain is reputed to have said, "The only two certainties in life are death and taxes." He may have said it, but he didn't originate it. The line comes from a letter Benjamin Franklin wrote to Jean Baptiste Le Roy.

—⟋⟍—

"**T**hose who sacrifice freedom for safety deserve neither." Another pithy comment attributed to Thomas Jefferson, the actual quote is, "Those who would give up essential Liberty, to purchase a little temporary Safety, deserve neither Liberty nor Safety," and it was said by Benjamin Franklin in 1755.

—⟋⟍—

Among his many memorable observations, Harry Truman, while musing about a life in politics, is reputed to have said, "If you can't take the heat, get out of the kitchen." But he didn't create the dissuasion; he was merely quoting his friend and military aide, General Harry Vaughan.

—⟋⟍—

"**T**hat government is best that governs least," a conviction credited to Thomas Jefferson, was actually written by Henry David Thoreau, in the first paragraph of his political essay "On the Duty of Civil Disobedience." However, Thoreau presented the phrase in quotes and called it a "motto," which authorities believe almost certainly referred to the literary-political periodical, the *United States Magazine and Democratic Review*, for which editor John L. O'Sullivan created the maxim, "The best government is that which governs least."

—⟋⟍—

Yes, Emerson did write, in his well-known essay "Self-Reliance," "Consistency is the hobgoblin of small minds," but that, like many promotional advertisements citing critics' laudatory comments, is only part of the quote. What he said was, "A foolish consistency is the hobgoblin of little minds, adored by little statesmen and philosophers and divines. With consistency a great soul has simply nothing to do." Thus, he wasn't asserting that consistency replaces thinking in small people, but that over-rigidity prevented creative thinking.

—⁂—

Mark Twain never said, "Everybody talks about the weather, but nobody does anything about it." It was written by journalist Charles Dudley Warner, Twain's collaborator on the novel *The Gilded Age* and attributed to an unnamed "well-known American writer." Twain denied it was him.

—⁂—

Dissent is the highest form of patriotism," is an aphorism credited to Thomas Jefferson. However, the quote is not two hundred years old; it is not even twenty years old. It is a statement by historian and social activist Howard Zinn, author of *A People's History of the United States*, and was said in about the year 2002.

—⁂—

Charles Boyer, as Pepe le Moko in the 1938 film *Algiers*, is remembered as trying to entice Hedy Lamarr with the line, "Come with me to the Casbah." He never said it, but the line stayed with him for the rest of his career—a signature piece of dialogue for mimics who imitated him.

—m—

In the first of Edgar Rice Burroughs' Tarzan novels, the 1914 *Tarzan of the Apes*, the wild man of the jungle is reputed to say, "Me Tarzan, you Jane." But he doesn't. Nor does he say it in the 1932 film adaptation of the novel. Rather, when Jane tries to explain the use of "me" and "you," he finally signifies his understanding when he points to himself and says, "Tarzan," and then points to her and says, "Jane." Then pointing alternately, he says, "Tarzan, Jane. Tarzan, Jane."

—m—

Sigmund Freud is said to have written, "Dreams are the royal road to the unconscious." Not quite. What Freud did write, in his landmark book *The Interpretation of Dreams*, was "The interpretation of dreams is the royal road to a knowledge of the unconscious activities of the mind."

—∭—

It is recounted that Paul Revere rode through the countryside alerting the colonists that "the British are coming." But such a warning is highly unlikely in that the colonists at that time all considered themselves British.

—∭—

Nowhere in his four novels and fifty-six short stories about Sherlock Holmes does author Arthur Conan Doyle have Holmes say, "Elementary, Dr. Watson."

—∭—

And no matter how often you watch the film *Casablanca*, you will never hear Bogey say to Dooley Wilson, "Play it again, Sam." Ilsa (Ingrid Bergman) does say, "Play it once, Sam, for old times' sake," and afterward, "Play it, Sam, play 'As Time Goes By.'" Still later, Rick (Bogart) tells his piano player, "You played it for her, you can play it for me." But never does he utter, "Play it again, Sam."

—∭—

SECTION THREE:

THE PUNDITS

To do justice to the subject at hand, it seems appropriate to end with some choice words from the experts, those persons who serve in responsible positions with years of relevant experience, leaders in their respective fields, well trained, well educated, quoted for their perspicacious insight, known throughout the world . . . and above all, WRONG!

"Who the Hell wants to hear actors talk?"

—H. B. Warner,
executive of Warner Brothers Pictures, 1927

"I cannot imagine any condition which could cause this ship to founder. I cannot conceive of any vital disaster happening to the vessel. Modern shipbuilding has gone beyond that."

—E. I. Smith,
captain of the *Titanic*, 1912

"The industrial condition of the United States is absolutely sound."

—Charles E. Mitchell,
Chairman of National City Bank,
September 20, 1929, one month before the crash

"The book has too much plot and not enough story."

—Sam Goldwyn

"When more and more people are thrown out of work, unemployment results."

—President Calvin Coolidge

"We must not be misled to our own detriment to assume that the untried machine can displace the proved and tried horse."

—Major General John H. Herr,
in 1938, talking about the tank in battlefield strategy

"I think there is a world market for about five computers."

—Thomas J. Watson,
IBM, 1958

"The atomic bomb will not go off, and I speak as an expert on explosives."

—Admiral W. Leahy to President Truman, 1945

"No generality is any damned good. And that includes this one."

—General William Tecumseh Sherman

"The depression has ended . . . In July, up we go."

—Dr. Julius Klein,
Assistant Secretary of Commerce,
June 9, 1931

"The picture will be a colossal flop."

—William Flanagan,
in a *New York Magazine* article,
"An Encounter with 'Close Encounters,'"
October 31, 1977

"The machines [airplanes] will eventually be fast, they will be used in sport. But they are not to be thought of as commercial carriers."

—*Popular Sciences Monthly*,
March 1904

"Verbosity leads to unclear, inarticulate things."

—Vice President Dan Quayle,
November 30, 1988

"It may be years—not in my time—before a woman will become prime minister."

—Margaret Thatcher, 1974

"Man will never reach the moon."

—Lee De Forest,
leading inventor of radio and telephonic
equipment, and father of sound films, 1957

"Who would want to see a play about an unhappy traveling salesman? Too depressing."

—Cheryl Crawford,
Broadway producer of several plays,
turning down an offer to produce
Death of a Salesman

" . . . ridiculous tricks of a ventriloquist. . . . It is quite impossible that the noble organs of human speech could be replaced by ignoble, senseless metal."

—Jean Bouillaud,
member of the French Academy of Sciences,
after seeing a demonstration of Edison's
new phonograph, September 30, 1878

"Louis Pasteur's theory of germs is ridiculous fiction."

—Pierre Pachet,
Professor of physiology at Toulouse, 1872

" . . . the automobile has practically reached the limit of its development . . ."

—*Scientific American*, January 2, 1909

"I think anybody who doesn't think I'm smart enough to handle this job is underestimating."

—President George Bush,
in *U.S. News and World Report*, April 3, 2008

"Can't act. Can't sing. Balding. Can dance a little."
—MGM exec about Fred Astaire's screen test

"There is no reason anyone would want a computer in their home."
—Ken Olsen, President and Founder,
Digital Equipment Corp., 1977

On December 10, 1903, the *New York Times* ran an article discussing the futility of men attempting to fly; one week later, the Wright Brothers made their historic first successful flight at Kitty Hawk, North Carolina.

"With over 50 foreign cars already on sale here, the Japanese auto industry isn't likely to carve out a big slice of the U.S. market."
—*BusinessWeek*, August 2, 1968

"Well, I learned a lot. You'd be surprised; they're all separate countries."
—President Ronald Reagan,
returning from a trip to Latin America

"There is not the lightest indication that nuclear energy will ever be obtainable. It would mean that the atom would have to be shattered at will."
—Albert Einstein, 1932

"We don't like their sound. Groups of guitars are on the way out."
—Decca executive, rejecting the Beatles, 1962

"I am not a crook. . . . I have never obstructed justice."
—Richard M. Nixon,
in an interview with Associated Press editors,
November 17, 1973

"It's hard for us, without being flippant, to even see a scenario within any kind of realm of reason that would see us losing one dollar in any of those transactions."
—Joseph A. Cassano,
American International Group executive, August 2007,
one month before the world's largest insurer
declared bankruptcy (the *New York Times*,
September 29, 2008, p. 1)

"[Lee] De Forest has said in many newspapers and over his signature that it would be possible to transmit human voice across the Atlantic before many years . . . absurd and deliberately misleading statements . . ."
—District Attorney trying De Forest for fraud, 1913

"A low vote turnout is an indication of fewer people going to the polls."
—Vice President Dan Quayle

"This 'telephone' has too many shortcomings to be seriously considered as a means of communication."
—Western Union memo, 1876

"Ruth made a big mistake when he gave up pitching."
—Tris Speaker, 1921

"It is highly unlikely that an airplane, or fleet of them, could ever successfully sink a fleet of Navy vessels under battle conditions."

—Franklin Delano Roosevelt,
when assistant secretary of the navy, 1922

"No matter what happens, the U.S. Navy is not going to be caught napping."

—Frank Knox,
U.S. secretary of the navy, on December 4,
1941, three days before the Japanese
air attack on Pearl Harbor

"My personal desire would be to prohibit entirely the use of alternating currents. They are unnecessary as they are dangerous."

—Thomas A. Edison, 1889

"I don't see much future for the Americans . . . it's a decayed country."

—Adolf Hitler, 1942

"The abolition of pain in surgery is a chimera. . . . 'Knife' and 'pain' are two words in surgery that must forever be associated in the consciousness of the patient."

—Leading surgeon Alfred Velpeau, 1839

"While theoretically and technically television may be feasible, commercially and financially it is an impossibility."

—Lee De Forest, pioneer of sound transmission inventions

"For the second time in our history, a British Prime Minister has returned from Germany bringing peace with honor. I believe it is peace for our time."

—Prime Minister Neville Chamberlain,
September 30, 1938, upon returning to London after
a Munich conference with Hitler, Mussolini,
and Édouard Daladier. Eleven months later,
on September 1, 1939, Hitler's forces invaded
Poland, setting off World War II.

"Rarely is the question asked, 'Is our children learning?'"

—President George W. Bush,
Florence, S.C., January 11, 2000

And one final scenario from our own homegrown social analyst cum philosopher cum cultural observer cum sage: "When you get to the fork in the road, take it."

—so advises Yogi Berra

And that's the last word from the experts!

END NOTE

So there you have it. We've looked at several common beliefs, some no doubt you, dear reader, have carried with you for who knows how long. And we've seen how easily we've been misled and how frequently we've been duped—by friends, teachers, the media, the experts, and even our parents.

Is there a moral to this story? Not likely. But it does suggest that we keep a wary eye, and reconfirm everything. It was Cicero (in *De Divinatione* II.xiii) who admonished us, "One does not have to believe everything that one hears." Perhaps there's some truth in the old saw: Believe nothing of what you hear, and only half of what you see. You may die an old skeptic, but you're much less likely to be taken in.

"It is not disbelief that is dangerous to our society,
it is belief."
—G. B. Shaw, Preface to *Androcles and the Lion*